Youth Work and Faith
Debates, Delights and Dilemmas

Edited by

Mark K. Smith, Naomi Stanton and Tom Wylie

Russell House Publishing

First published in 2015 by:
Russell House Publishing Ltd.
58 Broad Street
Lyme Regis
Dorset DT7 3QF

Tel: 01297-443948
Fax: 01297-442722
e-mail: help@russellhouse.co.uk
www.russellhouse.co.uk

British Library Cataloguing-in-publication Data:
A catalogue record for this book is available from the British Library.

ISBN: 978-1-905541-86-7

Cover photo: TPopova/istockphoto.com
Typeset by TW Typesetting, Plymouth, Devon
Printed by IQ Laserpress, Aldershot

About Russell House Publishing

Russell House Publishing aims to publish innovative and valuable materials to help
managers, practitioners, trainers, educators and students.

Our full catalogue covers: families, children and young people; engagement and
inclusion; drink, drugs and mental health; textbooks in youth work and social work;
workforce development.

Full details can be found at www.russellhouse.co.uk
and we are pleased to send out information to you by post. Our contact details are on
this page.

Contents

About the Editors and the Contributors

Mark K. Smith is Rank Research Fellow at YMCA George Williams College, London.

Naomi Stanton is a Lecturer in Youth Work at YMCA George Williams College, London.

Tom Wylie is former CEO of the National Youth Agency.

Shelley Marsh is Executive Director of Limmud, a global Jewish learning organisation.

Jon Jolly is Business Manager at Arun Community Church, Littlehampton.

Sughra Ahmed is Programmes Manager at the Woolf Institute, Cambridge.

Nigel Pimlott is Deputy CEO of Frontier Youth Trust.

Sarah-Jane Page is a Lecturer in Sociology at Aston University.

Pete Harris is a Senior Lecturer in Youth and Community Work at Newman University, Birmingham.

Helen Bardy is a Senior Lecturer in Youth and Community Work at Newman University, Birmingham.

Pauline Grace is Senior Lecturer and Programme Leader of the MA in Youth and Community Work at Newman University, Birmingham.

John Holmes is the former Programme Leader of Youth and Community Work at Newman University and Westhill College, Birmingham.

Mike Seal is Principal Lecturer and Programme Leader of Youth and Community Work at Newman University, Birmingham.

Phil Henry is Director of the Multi-Faith Centre at the University of Derby.

Bernard Davies is an independent trainer and consultant.

Maxine Green is Principal and Chief Executive at YMCA George Williams College, London.

Jess Bishop is Course Director of the BA (Hons) in Youth Work at Coventry University.

CHAPTER 1

Introduction: Different Traditions – Common Themes?

Mark Smith, Naomi Stanton and Tom Wylie

Following recent decline in state-sponsored youth work provision alongside growth in the faith-based sectors, thinking about youth work and faith is crucial, both to those working in faith-based settings and those working with them as partners or funders. This volume draws on the debates, delights and dilemmas of the relationship between youth work and faith. It is informed by a range of perspectives, from specific faith traditions as well as considering the cross-cutting issues.

Since the 1990s, the balance of youth work provision has markedly shifted so that by the early twenty-first century it was claimed that, in England and Wales, more full-time youth workers were now employed in faith settings than secular ones (Brierley, 2003: 12; Green, 2006: 3). This text aims to address some of the underlying tensions within faith-based work and to embrace the contribution made by the faith-based sector to the youth work field. Whilst using the term 'the faith-based sector' to discuss the many expressions of youth work that come under the umbrella of faith, we note that the faith sector, like youth work overall, is not homogeneous; indeed, it incorporates a whole spectrum of missions, values, affiliations and interventions. Moreover, there are many people 'of faith' who work in the 'secular' sector and, increasingly, vice versa; particularly, as religious organisations have taken over previously local authority run youth clubs under the Government's Big Society agenda and its concurrent austerity drive. Whilst we recognise this text is particularly timely in the current political climate, with the Government arguably using the faith sector as a device to shrink the state (which is, indeed, a thread of the chapter by Nigel Pimlott), we are keen to emphasise that tensions may emerge from the faith sector allowing itself to be embraced by the objectives and funding of the state.

The chapter authors approach the issues from academic and practitioner perspectives and the book covers a range of pertinent topics, including some of the 'tricky issues' such as sexuality, death and indoctrination. We hope that the book will open up debate between the faith-based and wider youth work sectors, recognising the field in its current form and the issues and opportunities we face as we approach a new era in youth work policy and practice.

The book begins by looking at three specific faith traditions with established youth work narratives; these being Jewish, Christian and Muslim. The next three chapters of the book consider some of the cross cutting issues for faith-based youth work from the perspectives of research and theory, these being involvement with civil society, discussions of sex and sexuality, and the issue of indoctrination. The text then considers the notion of interfaith integration, both in the context of training for youth workers of different faiths and none (Bardy et al.) and in the youth work setting itself (Henry). The three final chapters of the book take a more personal and practice-related approach to reflecting on the meaning of faith and spirituality in youth work. Through personal reflections and experiences, Bernard Davies considers the role of doubt in youth work and Maxine Green offers some thoughts on the use of our 'spiritual self' as a tool for practice. Jess Bishop then considers the oft-neglected topic of working with young people on the issue of death and dying.

Dialogue

Despite the range of issues and perspectives covered, there are common themes that emerge from the chapters that offer some key implications for faith-based youth work and for others in working alongside faith-based youth workers. Perhaps the most common and pertinent of these themes is that of the need for young people to have space for dialogue – in the form of one-to-one conversations and group discussions on a plethora of issues from the role of faith in their lives to some of the harder to broach issues such as sex, doubt and death. In her chapter on Jewish Youth Work, Shelley Marsh explains how conversations can be 'mutually transformative' for young people and leaders. Sarah-Jane Page, in chapter six, emphasises how young people need space for open discussion, as opposed to uncompromising dogma, on issues of sex and sexuality in relation to faith. In their chapter on integrated faith-based and secular training for youth work, Helen Bardy and her colleagues promote dialogue both between different faith traditions and between faith and non-faith practitioners.

Reflection

Another common theme throughout the text is that youth work is a site for critical reflection. In the cases of Davies and Green, their chapters encourage reflection on a deeply personal level; Green, in utilising our own spiritual selves, and Davies, in his personal narrative of embracing doubt. Similarly, Bishop encourages youth workers to reflect on their role in supporting young people who encounter grief or illness. In his chapter addressing the issue of indoctrination, Harris challenges us to reflect philosophically on the values of faith-based youth work. Other chapters promote young people's reflection through critical dialogue within their religious communities, such as Page's research highlighting the need for discussions about sex, as mentioned above, and Henry's research on inter-faith work with young people which supports the need for reflective dialogue between young people of different faith communities.

Agenda

The text also draws out some of the tensions that can exist between the agenda of the religious organisation and that of the young people. This tension is not restricted to faith-based youth work; the wider sector is engaged in an ongoing debate as to whether youth work provision should start from the concerns of young people or from easily measurable pre-defined targets set by funders and policy-makers. Jon Jolly, in his discussion of Christian youth work, emphatically notes that the purpose of such work can be entirely social and, in some cases, not reflect a religious agenda at all. In reflecting on her research about the needs of young British Muslims, Sughra Ahmed offers the Muslim Youth Helpline as an example of a service that is entirely premised on the needs and concerns of the young people. She explains how the helpline was created in response to the number of young Muslims who needed space to discuss repressed concerns, particularly on 'taboo' issues. This supports the findings of Page's research, that young people need space to discuss and explore issues relating to sex for themselves rather than being exposed to a rigid religious agenda.

Participation

As in most youth work texts, young people's participation is an undercurrent of all the chapters, from their participation in some of the critical reflection and dialogue already outlined or their participation within their communities.

Ahmed emphasises citizenship and belonging from the perspective of young Muslims who seek to cultivate an active British identity without compromising their religious loyalties. Marsh outlines the activist foundations of Jewish youth work as well as the participation of Jewish young people today within their faith communities and on an international scale. Pimlott offers a more general overview of the role of faith-based youth work in civil society.

Spirituality

The book moves beyond focusing on individual faith traditions in order to reflect more widely on the relationship between youth work and faith. Stemming from this is an understanding that spirituality as an aspect of youth work is something wider than simply adherence to a particular religious faith. This is drawn out, perhaps most explicitly, by Green, Davies, Bishop and Bardy et al. in their respective chapters which do not focus exclusively on youth work that is facilitated by those who belong to a particular religious community.

Concluding remarks

The themes of this volume such as youth work as a space for young people's discussion, reflection, critical thought and active participation are values that most youth workers would subscribe to, and not exclusive to the faith sector. They appear as key principles in the theory and practice of youth work and informal education more generally (see, for example, Jeffs and Smith, 2005). The tensions between upholding these principles and dealing with an organisational agenda are also just as present in secular as in faith-based youth work. These shared values and struggles offer common ground for the field to come together upon. We hope that this text opens up dialogue between those who champion youth work from different faith traditions and between faith-based and non-faith youth work. As a field we are stronger together than we are fragmented – recognising the diversity and richness of our practices yet embracing common values.

References

Brierley, D. (2003) *Joined Up: An Introduction to Youthwork and Ministry.* Cumbria: Spring Harvest Publishing/Authentic Lifestyle.

Green, M. (2006) *A Journey of Discovery: Spirituality and Spiritual Development in Youth Work.* Leicester: The National Youth Agency.

Jeffs, T. & Smith, M. K. (2005) *Informal Education – Conversation, Democracy and Learning.* (revised edn.) Nottingham: Educational Heretics Press.

CHAPTER 2

On Renewing and Soaring: Transformation and Actualisation in Contemporary Jewish Youth Provision

Shelley Marsh

Whilst for outsiders, the Jewish community appears tightly knit, historically, Jewish immigrants came to the UK from a variety of lands, and many had originated from countries where mainstream society was not open to Jews. In their communities of origin, the majority of young people would have found work, life direction and even a spouse through extended family units and communal links. Jewish youth provision has existed in Britain since the nineteenth century, following Jewish immigration into the UK. Jewish youth clubs were established to create a safe space for Jewish immigrant young people. Jewish youth club managers, many of whom had already been resident in the UK for years, or who were UK born, were the ideal people to offer the newly arrived immigrants both practical advice and words of experience to ease the young people into life in Britain, rather than their parents and extended families, who were themselves struggling to acclimatise.

Jewish young people also wanted to meet other Jewish young people who were transitioning from one lifestyle to another. Following the Biblical injunction to honour one's father and mother, young people would rarely go against their parents' wishes and immigrant parents were cautious in allowing their children to mix with non-Jews, fearing anti-Semitism. The Jewish youth club allayed parental concerns as well as offering young people social interaction with peers, an extended community and a place where young people could learn, in an informal setting, how to settle into being British whilst keeping their Jewish identity intact. These young people 'had to harmonise Englishness and Jewishness and on no abstract, philosophical level' (Bunt, 1975: 13).

Lily Montagu, in her 1904 paper 'The girl in the background', explored the difficulties of working class girls, who faced unequal pay and poor working conditions (Spence, 1999). She hoped that Jewish youth work would empower young women who were particularly marginalised. Montagu was critical of Jewish youth work that emphasised leisure-time, since she believed it was essential to develop a deeper level of personal development through activism.

> They try to make their girls conduct themselves well in clubs . . . [However,] if the girls work for less than a living wage . . . they are not likely to become the strong, self controlled women whom we desire the clubs to train.

> (Montagu, 1904, cited in Spence, 1999: web)

Jewish youth work therefore evolved with varied objectives and methodologies. Socialisation, politicisation, activism, education and escapism were all components of early Jewish youth work. Its early success was that Jewish young people were attracted by the activities on offer, parents were confident that their children were safe from outside influences of which they were fearful; therefore Jewish young people regularly attended the increasing number of Jewish youth clubs.

Jewish clubs were incredibly popular over many years and remained so until the late 1990s, with a smaller, but highly engaged, minority, attending Jewish youth movements. However, youth work practice has altered greatly in the past twenty years, as a result of a major communal shift towards increased enrolment at Jewish secondary schools. In turn, the need for socialisation has diminished and Jewish youth work in the UK has increasingly focused on issues of identity, connection to Israel, spirituality and enculturalisation. Since the late twentieth century, there have been greater numbers of young people engaging in Jewish youth movements alongside a steep decline in Jewish youth club participation.

This chapter will outline how youth work has been expressed within the British Jewish community,* exploring areas of change in Jewish youth work practice. Section One will give a brief overview of the three principal youth work models active within the mainstream British Jewish Community, whilst

---

* This chapter does not include research into the ultra Orthodox (Chareidi) Jewish community.

Section Two will examine aspects of the current youth movement model, exploring the historical impact and contemporary challenges facing Jewish youth provision in twenty-first century Britain.

The transformative nature of informal education and its impact on all young people, both as participants as well as on the leaders themselves, has been held in esteem in the Jewish community. Whilst much of Jewish youth work takes place in the UK, there are a number of programmes which are designed to strengthen Jewish identity development including many international programmes. Within the Jewish youth work sector, visiting Israel as the spiritual homeland and religious centre of Judaism is recognised as a central part of Jewish identity development. The British Jewish community openly discusses and explores the nuances and complexities of the modern day State of Israel (termed as 'hugging and wrestling' with Israel by Gringas, 2004) with its young people, as well as reflecting on their connections to Judaism and Jewish peoplehood.

Section One: Three Models of Jewish Youth Work

Jewish youth work in the UK has a rich and varied history of developing young people through informal education. Through a diverse range of Jewish youth movements, organisations and clubs, young people have accessed sports, arts, education, educational travel and informal spaces to meet, interact with and learn from their peers since the nineteenth century (Bunt, 1975: 105). A leading figure in the establishment of this model was Basil Henriques, known as The Gaffer, (1890–1961) who not only raised funds to purchase a building but set out both an organisational and philosophical ethos of Jewish youth work (Infed, undated). Henriques and many other Jewish youth workers actively encouraged young people to volunteer in work with younger children as part of the youth club experience. Many of those in leadership roles within the Jewish community will attribute their ongoing engagement in community work, either as a lay leader or a Jewish communal professional, to the empowerment they received as a young person. Taking on a leadership role at the age of 13–14 was, and remains, common practice in Jewish youth leadership or 'hadracha'.*

---

* Hadracha – translated from the Hebrew term 'the way' implies that walking alongside or slightly ahead of one's peers, is the appropriate term for Jewish leadership. Hadracha courses are facilitated in all Jewish youth movements with this terminology underpinning the key experience of peer leadership.

Jewish youth clubs: a social acculturation model

The traditional focus of the Jewish youth clubs was socialisation, creating spaces for Jewish young people to meet and socialise with Jewish peers. The youth clubs offered cultural activities five nights per week for different age groups. Many of these received government and/or local authority funding, as well as additional funding from the Jewish community itself. Organisations such as Maccabi GB and The Association of Jewish Youth provided training and support to the field of Jewish youth work. The notion of youth empowerment and peer leadership was present in the Jewish youth clubs but club leaders also followed mainstream youth work models: engaging in conversations with young people, experiential learning and social development. Lily Montagu wrote:

> A club worker must enter on her career in the learning spirit. She must not attempt to foist her standards on the girls among whom she intends to work. She must study their standards, and exchange her point of view with theirs.
>
> (Montagu, 1954: 24)

In the Jewish youth clubs, young people would typically sit on committees which were democratically elected by their peers, working together to form the content of the youth clubs' programmes. Music, drama and sports groups were popular and young people would organise tournaments, shows and galas with the support of professional adult youth workers. The exploration of Jewish themes through the arts and sport gave great scope to the development of talent but the main aim was to allow young Jewish people to come together to enjoy themselves. Building friendships with other Jewish young people and gaining confidence through social activities were the main attractions to these clubs for young people in the British Jewish community. Spiritual and religious development did not receive much formal emphasis although, in the majority of clubs, Jewish festivals would have been recognised and celebrated. Activities ran from Sunday to Thursday, with no provision on Friday evening or Saturday (Sabbath), since that would have conflicted with synagogue activities. Youth workers, who were considered to be acting as role models, led the majority of clubs. Qualified youth workers were trained to engage young people through activities which were entertaining although not necessarily educationally demanding. However, the Jewish youth clubs did not exist without critique. In 1975, Sidney Bunt wrote:

Unless the Jewish youth service breaks free from it own past . . . it will run a serious risk of disintegration . . . before it reaches its centenary in 1983 . . . What may be more appropriate to the sort of informal Jewish youth work of the future would be that a greater number of structures . . . could be confidently handed over to young people.

(Bunt, 1975: 208)

Jewish youth workers, many with youth work qualifications, were supported by well trained volunteers and older young people who were keen to offer support and advice to younger youth club members. Over the past twenty years, the desire to take on voluntary leadership roles within Jewish youth clubs has slowly dissipated and, coupled with diminishing numbers of children attending youth clubs on a weekly basis, gradually, other structures have developed. Bunt was correct in his understanding that the success of Jewish youth work was in confidently handing it over to young people. The Jewish youth movements are managed and run by and for young people, as the remainder of this chapter will highlight.

Jewish youth movements: a model of peer leadership

During the early part of the twentieth century, a number of peer-led, ideologically focussed Jewish youth organisations established themselves in the UK as well as in Jewish communities across Europe. The youth movements were initially developed in response to changes in European Jewish experience. The primary focus was, and continues to be, on a wide range of ideological positions, aiming to develop a strong connection to Judaism and the land of Israel as the Jewish spiritual homeland. Section Two of this chapter will explore the youth movement model in greater detail.

Informal education in Jewish schools: a model of adaptation

Over the past thirty years, increasing numbers of Jewish young people have enrolled in Jewish schools thus spending a significant amount of their time within a Jewish educational environment. One significant effect of this shift has been that young people are making Jewish friends at school, resulting in them (or their parents) no longer having the same level of interest in attending Jewish youth clubs for the purpose of forming Jewish friendship groups.

Young people having access to a 'Jewish atmosphere' was important to Jewish parents in the past (Bunt, 1975: 84–7). An outcome of (and indeed the attraction of) Jewish schooling is that young people remain within a Jewish environment, enabling them to form Jewish friendship circles in school, thus appearing to undermine the need previously served by the youth clubs. While lack of research makes it difficult to link the rise of Jewish schooling with the decline of Jewish youth clubs with certainty, there has been profound change to the youth clubs over the same period of time, with a less pronounced effect on youth movements. The youth movements have continued to attract young people, particularly to residential events, which are facilitated during school holidays.

Jewish secondary schools employ informal educators, who are responsible for educational experiences around Jewish festivals, Sabbath residential activities and maintaining a cohesive Jewish ethos throughout the school. The majority of Jewish schools will teach Jewish Studies alongside the National Curriculum as well as at GCSE, AS and A level. In many schools, the informal educator role is managed as part of the 'formal' Jewish studies department. In most schools, pastoral care is separated from the informal educators and is managed by school counsellors, SENCo staff and pastoral managers, along with Rabbis, who work as a multi disciplinary team in supporting young people to engage in the types of conversations that are characteristic of youth work.

Jewish schools are overt in their desire to increase Jewish knowledge, literacy and understanding in their students. Prayer, Jewish traditions, learning about festivals and learning to read Hebrew (the written language of prayer and study) are covered in the realm of the formal curriculum as well as through synagogue attendance and the home. The role of the informal educator in the Jewish school is to support and extend Jewish experiences for the students. Schools have increasingly recognised the need to support the large numbers of young people in their cultural identity and spiritual development. A significant number of Jewish Studies teachers and heads of Jewish Studies are ex-movement workers or graduates of the youth movements and are attempting to replicate for the young people in their schools, the transformative experience they received. However, within the formal school environment, these informal educators lack an ideological framework that is characteristic of youth work values and they therefore face challenges in reconstructing youth-led activities.

Section Two: The Youth Movement Model – Impact and Challenges in the Twenty-first Century

The significant difference between the experiences offered by the Jewish youth clubs and the youth movements is the transformative intent of the latter. The youth movements are based on a model of transformational education, which can be seen as one reason for the endurance of Jewish youth movements in the UK despite the decline of Jewish youth clubs.

Mezirow describes this transformative education as:

> . . . *learning that induces more far-reaching change in the learner than other kinds of learning . . . which shape the learner and produce a significant impact, or paradigm shift, which affects the learner's subsequent experiences.*
>
> (Mezirow, 1981: 3–24)

He highlights the importance of transformative education as 'filtering' one's life experiences and explores how one might then interpret meaning.

> *Meaning perspectives are acquired passively during childhood and youth . . . the transformation that occurs through experience during adulthood. They operate as perceptual filters that determine how an individual will organize and interpret the meaning of his/her life's experiences.*
>
> (Mezirow, 1997: 5–12)

This is a fundamental part of what Jewish informal education attempts to achieve in both participants and leaders. Fostering spaces for young people and young adults to think through their own lives, positively impacting on the thought processes of others and developing role models who can develop mentoring relationships are vital outcomes of the peer leadership structure found in British Jewish youth work.

Enabling spiritual intelligence

Within the Jewish youth movements there is an emphasis on the development of spiritual intelligence, something not clearly evident in the other models explored above.* Each Jewish youth movement gives consideration to prayer, Sabbath observance, blessings for food and giving thanks to God. Zohar and

---

* Some synagogue-based youth groups have formally developed this area to a much greater extent.

Marshall explain that:

> *To experience 'the spiritual' means to be in touch with some larger, deeper, richer whole that puts our present limited situation into a new perspective. It is to have a sense of 'something beyond', of 'something more' that confers added meaning and value on where we are now . . . a sense that our actions are part of some greater universal process.*
>
> (Zohar and Marshal, 2004: 18)

This sentiment could have been expressed by many twenty-first century Jewish youth movement leaders, who lead ethical boycotts, encourage their membership to address issues of inequality and believe wholeheartedly that these are ways of ensuring Jewish values are adhered to and transmitted as a live educational message. Many Jewish youth movements will only purchase foods, camping equipment or merchandise based on ethical procurement. One Jewish youth movement states that:

> *We all inherit the tradition and believe that it is a living and dynamic system . . . We seek to imbue our members with the knowledge and skills to develop a love for Jewish practice and learning.*
>
> (Noam, 2013: web)

Another Jewish youth movement, expresses its ideological and religious beliefs as:

> *. . . made up of a combination of traditional and more creative elements. Shabbat is a truly out-of-this-world experience, made special by you putting your heart and soul into creating a fabulous atmosphere.*
>
> (RSY-Netzer, undated: web)

The notion of spiritual intelligence (as defined by Zohar and Marshal, 2004) resonates through the practical outcomes of the Jewish youth movements such as peer leadership, collective responsibility, social action and volunteering. Whilst the term spiritual intelligence is not one that Jewish youth work associates itself with, it is evident that the youth work currently happening in the British Jewish community expresses exceptionally high levels of emotional, social and spiritual intelligence.

Transformative learning processes

The majority of Jewish youth movements maintain similar structures to engage young Jewish people on their individual journeys. There are five identifiable stages in the process of Jewish informal education that a young person goes through, by their participation in a Jewish youth movement:

1. **Initial Engagement:** Socialisation into a peer group which is activity-based with the same group of young people every week/month. Activities vary and encourage peer leadership in designing and delivering the activity itself. Groups within each movement will meet in a variety of national locations, some will be based in synagogues and some will not. The building and location is often utilised for convenience only and often does not play a part in the planning or outcome of activity. This differs from the desire to create a 'home from home' which was part of the Jewish youth club culture.

2. **Developmental:** Residential activities build the individual groups and offer greater accessibility to those who do not attend regular weekly/monthly meetings. Opportunities are opened to participants and to leaders. In a completely youth focussed environment, the ideological position of the movement, a focus of Jewish culture, heritage, people-hood and practice can be explored through an intensive educational process. The residential experience features throughout the world in Jewish informal education programmes. Responsibilities around food preparation, site cleanliness, individual and collective responsibility are crucial to the development of educational experiences within these residentials, often referred to as creating the 'hadracha (Jewish youth movement) bubble'.

3. **Transformative:** Residential activities have created structures for transformative learning to take place. Mezirow (1997) argues that transformative change requires new experiences that are outside of the individual's 'frame of reference'. Educational tours to sites of European Jewish heritage, or to Israel for participants aged 16 and 17, supported by undergraduate leaders are a key feature of the youth movements. 55% of each cohort of UK Jewish 16 year olds participate in Israel tours each summer. These Europe and Israel Tours are transformative for both leaders and participants, in differing ways. At age 16, the Israel Tour participants know, but do not fully appreciate, the magnitude of their role in the continuity of their Jewish community. Educational travel is the gateway to further engagement as young people are inspired to deepen their knowledge and involvement with the Jewish community. Following the tours, many become involved in leadership programmes, through the post-tour Jewish youth movement structures and will, in five years time, be leading Israel Tours for another cohort of 16 year olds.

   A key change in the transformative stage is from participant to stakeholder. The term stakeholder reiterates the importance of shared ownership that is fundamental to the continuity of the youth movements. The passion and commitment of the members that pick up the baton of leadership from one cohort to the next is the basis of moving from participation (as an Israel Tour participant) to a stakeholder leader. The stakeholder leaders debate and decide on the educational direction and development of the youth movement.

4a. **Aspirational (Gap Year):** Following the completion of school, and traditionally pre-university, participation in Gap Year programmes has given young people a structure for self-development, new skills and semi-independent living, as one movement explains:

> Your gap year is when you can devote specific time to Jewish learning . . . designed to help you make the most of that time. And you'll find that being on Gap Year is a learning experience itself – you'll grow as a person.

(Bnei Akiva, undated: web)

Upon returning from Gap Year, Jewish young people will generally attend university and will continue to volunteer for their youth movement in term breaks, supporting and leading younger members who are in the initial engagement and developmental stages. In their third year of university, approximately 70 students will volunteer as Tour leaders, influencing the young people who are the upcoming generation of leaders both for their youth movements and the British Jewish Community. As Emeritus Chief Rabbi Sacks has noted:

> Not all of us have power. But we all have influence, whether we seek it or not. We make the people around us better or worse . . . That quiet leadership of influence seeks no power but it changes lives.

(Sacks, 2011: web)

For many years, Gap Year programmes have created an educational mechanism for Jewish Diaspora communities to send Jewish young people to Israel, deepening Jewish identities and connections to Jewish people-hood. Whilst some Jewish communities have seen stable participation levels on Gap Year programmes, the UK Jewish community has seen a decline in young people accessing these programmes. Tuition fees, parental pressures, the availability of competitively-priced innovative international programmes, and the increasing costs of Israel-based programmes are impacting on these educational and leadership opportunities, which the

Jewish youth movements along with the British Jewish community more generally, are only now addressing.

4b. **Aspirational stage (Tour leader):** For many leaders, volunteering to lead a tour is an opportunity to 'give back' to the youth movement and many will then choose to lead the youth movement itself a year or so later, following graduation from university. The Israel Tour leaders are trained within a communal structure, by Jewish youth work professionals, to understand their roles. They will work with peers within a core team, with additional professional support, throughout the duration of the tour itself, which lasts for approximately three weeks in the summer. The leadership training process, and subsequently leading a tour, is viewed as a key point in one's Jewish leadership journey. The screening and educational input given to Israel Tour leaders aims to increase the leadership potential seen in each leader. The In Defence of Youth Work campaign (IDYW) notes that within professional youth work practice a key element is:

> *[the] essential significance of the youth worker themselves, whose outlook, integrity and autonomy is at the heart of fashioning a serious yet humorous, improvisatory yet rehearsed educational practice with young people.*

(IDYW, 2009: web)

Israel Tour leaders have daily opportunities to engage in conversations with their participants. The tour, whilst intense, creates an ideal space for participants to have conversations with their young leaders. Jewish youth work flourishes in the Israel Tour environment, as young people and their young adult leaders, in a defined group setting, engage in meaningful conversations about Jewish learning; the ancient versus the modern; what it means to be a young Jewish person in the Diaspora; the complexities of contemporary Israeli society as well as mainstream youth work conversations which may explore issues such as: sexuality; equality; 'Does he fancy me?' and 'What will happen to the rest of my life if I fail my GCSEs?'

The Israel Tour is currently the 'Jewel in the Crown' of Jewish informal education, as both the gateway to further informal educational experiences but also a high point of the Jewish journey for both participants and leaders. The opportunities offered to both young adults as leaders and young people as participants through Tour and Gap Year experiences are noted throughout the Jewish community as being meaningful and transformative through experiential learning and exposure to role models.

5. **Actualisation:** Jewish youth movements are managed by sabbatical work-ers, who have been involved in the movement for a number of years. The sabbatical movement workers, generally university graduates, spend one to two years running the movement, in small teams of between two and five people. These movements are essentially run by intellectually driven young Jewish adults, who have been through an academic process and are often trying to apply their theoretical models of the world to the reality they now encounter. The majority of movement workers are ideologically driven and dedicated to giving their time to the youth movement that has given so much to them. They are given financial, educational, logistical and ideological responsibility for all the stages identified above. Through the democratic processes of the individual movements they are able to develop ideological positions, such as:

> *[The movement] believes in personal autonomy and opposes religious fundamentalism and coercion.*
>
> (Bnei Akiva, undated: web)

> *[The movement] seeks to be an engaged, literate, questioning, obser-vant, vibrant and caring Kehila (community), that is the driving force behind the [Jewish] Community and its future.*
>
> (Bnei Akiva, undated: web)

> *Our rabbis said long ago "You don't have to finish the job, but you can't say it's not your responsibility to make a start" (Ethics of the Fathers) and that sums up our approach . . . we hope you'll be inspired to go out and try to change the world too.*
>
> (RSY-Netzer, undated: web)

> *Many people through their time in [the movement] experience a change in values, beliefs and practice.*
>
> (Noam, 2013: web)

The process is as profound for the individual as for the movement itself, as one youth movement summarises:

> *The value is based around your own individual . . . journey, from a chanich/[participant], to a madatz/[learner], to a madrich/[leader] to a boger/et [graduate]. It is all about personal development.*
>
> (RSY-Netzer, undated: web)

Clearly the actualisation stage does have some limitations in that there are a restricted number of sabbatical positions available to lead the youth movement. Some young people who wish to take up those positions may not be elected into office. However, since the nature of Jewish youth work places such an emphasis on volunteering, many young people choose to retain their involvement with the movement even if they are not able to take up a formal leadership position. Structurally, Jewish informal education continues to expand and has been successful in creating wide-ranging capacity for voluntary leaders to take up lay leadership positions to offer support and guidance to the youth movements.

Table 2.1: Summary of the youth movements' pathway stages

Initial engagement:	• Weekly or monthly meetings, with an educational aim (participants from age 8+ for participants; leaders volunteering from age 14+). • Weekly or monthly social activities (participants from age 8+; leaders volunteering from age 14+).
Development:	• Residential weekend experiences (participants from age 8+, leaders from age 16+). • Week long winter and two week summer residential activity in the UK (participants will be from across age groups, leaders from age 16+).
Transformative:	• Month long educational summer tour of Israel/Europe for 16–17 year olds.
Aspirational:	• International Gap Year programmes for 18 year old participants. • Voluntary Tour leaders (aged 20–22) lead in teams of four.
Actualisation:	• Leading the youth movement: full-time sabbatical role (one or two years). • Fulfilment of the youth movement's ideological position through life choices.

Mutually transformative conversations

The importance of conversations with young people cannot be underestimated and it is the ability to have open conversations, the prominence and weighting given to those conversations that make the difference within a youth work context. For the Jewish thinker, Martin Buber, conversations can be mutually transformative.

> In the most powerful moments of dialogic, where in truth 'deep calls unto deep', it becomes unmistakably clear that it is not the wand of the individual or the social, but of a third which draws the circle around the happening. On the far side of the subjective, on this side of the objective, on the narrow ridge, where I and Thou meet, there is the realm of 'between'. Here the genuine third alternative is indicated,

*the knowledge of which will help to bring about the genuine person
again and to establish genuine community.*

(Buber, 1947: 65)

The impact of the mentoring relationship on both the mentor and the mentee
is highly significant in the development of Jewish identity. Youth work conversations are meaningful for all who participate in them. One is not a teacher and
the other a learner: the mutuality of the relationship as a device for deepening Jewish identity is impactful for *both* mentor and mentee. The importance
of mentors and role models as the key people in enhancing Jewish identity
development in young people is central (Marsh, 2006).

IDYW has explored the importance of conversations being at the heart of
professional youth work:

> . . . *conversations with young people which start from their concerns
> and within which both youth worker and young person are educated
> and out of which opportunities for new learning and experience can
> be created.*

(IDYW, 2009: web)

These informal conversations leave long lasting impressions on participants
and youth leaders. External to the Jewish secondary schools, many conversations with Jewish young people remain in the domain of sabbatical Jewish
youth workers. Social issues which young people face such as bullying,
disordered eating and substance abuse are areas which would have been
supported by youth work professionals and are now addressed by sabbatical
youth movement workers and informal educators in schools. As has been
identified above, the majority of movement workers graduate from university
education and begin a year in office, leading their youth organisations. With
approximately forty youth movement workers developing as a cohort across
the movements each year, these young adults are hard working and dedicated, but are relatively inexperienced in the complexities of young people's
social issues. They lack the training in youth work, and the professional experience of dealing with difficulties and then reflecting on how appropriately they
have handled these.

Conclusion

This chapter has surveyed the historic and current changes that have taken
place in youth work within the British Jewish community. Jeffs and Smith
define the distinctive aspects of youth work as including:

The relationship between the client or participant and the worker remains voluntary, with the former invariably retaining the right to both initiate any association with the worker and more importantly to terminate it . . . The work undertaken primarily has an educational purpose . . . The focus of the work is directed towards young people . . . Remove one and it becomes obvious that what is being observed may possess a resemblance to, but is unquestionably not, youth work.

(Jeffs and Smith, 1999: web)

Informal education in Jewish secondary schools does not offer the opportunity to opt out. Jewish enrichment programmes, modern Hebrew, and religious celebrations are a part of the established school timetable. The informal educators in Jewish schools adhere to the term 'informal education' and not 'youth work' and perhaps most importantly, are confident that the work undertaken with young Jewish people enhances their Jewish experiences. Additional residential weekends (usually over the Sabbath) are optional and schools report a high uptake on these optional activities. Informal education is a relatively new concept in Jewish secondary schools. There has been little research published in this area in the British Jewish community despite some consideration of informal education in formal settings in the wider youth work field over recent years. A longitudinal study is currently being undertaken and it may give further insight into the influence of Jewish informal education in schools.

More than thirty years ago, Bunt questioned the focus of Jewish youth work, as entertainment (socialisation) or education.

*If entertainers . . . we do not do well in that . . . If educators, we must decide whether **we** shall teach Jewish youth what **we** believe they should know, or whether our role is rather to help them learn what **they** themselves identify, with our help, as important and worth learning.*

(Bunt, 1975: 77)

The Jewish youth clubs existed on the basis that young people opted in, within a social and normative value but without any coercion or defined necessary outcome. The context of the Jewish youth club was initially that its members were empowered to develop personally and later, to explore their Jewish identity in any way they chose to do so. As such, the notion of transformation within Jewish youth work has some clear limitations, since the overall goal is to strengthen engagement and involvement within the Jewish community itself, whether in the Diaspora or in Israel, and not outside of it. Involvement in this context could be defined as part of a wide spectrum which includes elements such as ensuring that young people continue to marry within the faith, take on communal leadership positions, support Jewish communal organisations and, most recently, develop social entrepreneurship which is of benefit to both the Jewish and wider communities.

The Jewish youth movements align with the youth club model of empowerment and optional activities. With fewer regular weekly meetings happening throughout Jewish youth work, but an increasing number of young people attending residential activities, there are fewer adults who have experienced youth work placements which are external to their organisations, delivering face to face youth work. Undertaking a Youth and Community Work qualification is no longer necessary to taking on a professional role since Jewish youth work as a profession has been replaced, in the majority of settings, by youth movement workers. Informal educators in Jewish schools are also not generally qualified in youth work. The eminent educational thinker, Nel Noddings has identified that:

> Children are not alone in experiencing conflicts between needs and wants . . . The child should be allowed to express his unhappiness or fear, and the adult should respond with understanding and sympathy.
>
> (Noddings, 2003: 66–7)

To put it simply, the realm of experience in supporting young people's needs is limited by the youth movement workers' lack of skill and experience in 'responding with understanding and sympathy' (ibid.). As young adults, without extended formal youth work training, the sabbatical youth movement workers are often inexperienced in recognising the need for or engaging in more complex pastoral care.

Neither informal education in schools nor youth movements excel at creating regular spaces for youth work conversations. The defined outcomes that need to be achieved within a set time frame limit the opportunities for conversations that young people often require. Both schools and youth movements are task orientated, the former on the transfer of knowledge which can be assessed, the later on actualisation or leadership which are more definable measurements of success than the outcomes of youth work conversations. In a faith community with an excellent history in youth work, where young people were able to access youth workers who were experienced in supporting young people's social and cultural needs, there is a need for further cohesion in the creation of safe, non-judgemental spaces.

The scale of uptake of Jewish informal education in Jewish schools, Jewish youth movements and the remaining Jewish youth clubs is still significant. Approximately 8,000 Jewish young people in the UK will engage in some form of Jewish informal education each year.

The UK Jewish community has put in place a range of strategies to support the youth movement workers and aspirational leaders. This support includes training seminars; mentoring programmes; logistical and back office support; as well as intensive evaluation and assessment programmes which embed good practice and offer different perspectives by looking at social issues through an intrinsically faith-based lens. Educational content, which is engaging to young people and delivered by young people, is the model the British Jewish community currently maintains. It is holistic in its approach, combining Jewish values with mainstream contemporary youth work practice.

The Jewish community acknowledges the difficulties and challenges its young people face. The community remains committed to its future through its young people and continues to invest in their education, wellbeing and development, allowing them to 'renew their strength', and at times to 'soar on wings', perhaps recognising, as Isaiah prophesied, that:

> *Even youths grow tired and weary, and . . . stumble and fall; but those who hope in the Lord will renew their strength. They will soar on wings like eagles; they will run and not grow weary, they will walk and not be faint.*

> (Isaiah 40: 29–31, Jerusalem Bible, 2008)

References

Bnei Akiva (undated) 'Hachsara', http://bauk.org/hachshara.

Buber, M. (1947) *Between Man and Man*. New York: Routledge Classics.

Bunt, S. (1975) *Jewish Youth Work in Britain: Past, Present and Future*. London: Bedford Square Press.

Gringras, R. (2004) *Hugging and Wrestling – Alternative Paradigms for the Diaspora-Israel Relationship*. Makom. http://makomisrael.org/blog/hugging-and-wrestling.

In Defence of Youth Work (2009) *The Open Letter*. http://www.indefenceofyouthwork.org.uk/wordpress/?page_id=90

Infed (undated) *Basil Henriques and Boys' Club Work*. YMCA George Williams College. http://www.infed.org/thinkers/henriques.htm.

Jerusalem Bible (2008) Jerusalem: Koren Publishers.

Jeffs, T. and Smith, M.K. (1999) The Problem of 'Youth' For Youth Work. *Youth and Policy*, 62, 45–66. Also available in *the informal education archives*, http://www.infed.org/archives/youth.htm.

Marsh, S. (2006) Exploring the Development of Jewish Identity in Young People. *Youth and Policy,* 92, 47–57.

Mezirow, J. (1981) A Critical Theory of Adult Learning and Education. Adult Education Quarterly, *32, 3–24.*

Mezirow, J. (1997) Transformative Learning: Theory to Practice. *New Directions for Adult and Continuing Education,* 74, 5–12.

Montagu, L. (1954) *My Club and I.* London: Neville Spearman and Herbert Joseph.

RSY-Netzer (undated) *What We Believe.* http://www.rsy-netzer.org.uk/about-us/what-we-believe. html.

Noam (2013) *Ideology.* Masorti Youth. http://masortiyouth.org/noam/about-us/ideology/.

Noddings, N. (2003) *Happiness and Education.* New York: Cambridge University Press.

Sacks, J. (2011) *Thought for the Day.* Office of the Chief Rabbi. http://www.chiefrabbi.org/ ReadArtical1855.aspx.

Spence, J. (1999) *Lily Montagu, Girl's Work and Youth Work.* Infed. http://infed.org/mobi/ lily-montagu-girls-work-and-youth-work/.

Walker, P. (undated) *Jewish East End of London Photo Gallery and Commentary.* http://www. jewisheastend.com/basilhenriques.html.

Zohar, D. and Marshal, I. (2004) *Spiritual Capital – Wealth We Can Live By.* London: Bloomsbury Publishing.

CHAPTER 3

Christian Youth Work: Motive and Method

Jon Jolly

Defining what constitutes youth work has historically been a challenging task and 'a matter of sometimes fierce debate' (Davies, 2010: 1). While attempts have been made to categorise descriptions, characteristics, and values of the work (Smith, 1988) there is no definitive answer. Similarly, trying to define the breadth of Christian youth work with any clarity is almost impossible. Examples of practice from Christianity include Bible studies, sexual health work, sports projects, mentoring, targeted youth support, religious meetings, outdoor activities, inter-faith activities, and general youth clubs among others. So what can really be defined as Christian youth work? The only constant appears to be that the individuals or organisations running them have Christian values and beliefs from which they derive the purpose of their work.

Christians have long been involved in youth work practice and development. From its beginnings as a response to the needs of the poor in the late 1800s through to present day, there is a rich history of Christians pioneering educative work with young people (Smith,1999; Eagar, 1953). Churches still provide a huge range of activities for the wider community including youth work. Indeed, the faith-based sector has been the 'fastest growing part of the youth work field over recent years' (Stanton, 2013: 193). In the *More Than Sundays* report (Buttery and Telling, 2009: 3), it was found that 86% of churches provide activities for children, young people and families in the community, which suggests a possible 32,000 churches working across England alone to provide services in this context. Brierley (2000) estimated the church in England and Wales employed 7,900 full-time youth workers (more than were employed by the state at the time). In addition to the paid workforce, volunteers provide an average of 38 hours per church per week (Buttery and Telling, 2009: 3). Increasingly, following major cuts to services in local areas, many faith-based groups have started projects and services – notably food banks – and looked to support young people let down by the authorities (Atkinson-Small, 2012). However, with growing poverty, an aging population and the retention of young people in the schooling system up to age 18 there is some anecdotal evidence to suggest there is less emphasis on work with young people by some churches and faith organisations.

Over the same period, we reached a point where an expression of Christianity (or any other faith) in youth work was often viewed with suspicion or scepticism (Pugh, 1999: 9). The importance of faith was once clearly, if cautiously recognised in state-sponsored youth work (see, for example, HMSO, 1960: 38), yet the current National Occupational Standards now only briefly mention 'spiritual' as a value or belief (LSIS, 2012: 69) and the term 'spiritual' has itself been widely debated due to its ambiguous meaning (Green, 1999: 1). So is it right to be sceptical of Christians' religious motivation and wary of their practice?

To begin to answer this question, to understand the proliferation of Christian youth work and to examine its purpose and practice, we need to look at some of the beliefs held by those who profess the faith. With over 41,000 Christian denominations and groupings globally (Pew Research, 2011: 95) it would be impossible to accurately summarise the variety of beliefs and practices across the spectrum of Christian faith, so here we will refer to the general trends present in mainstream Christian churches in the UK (denominations including Anglican, Catholic, Baptist, Methodist, and other evangelical churches).

The motivations to work with young people

Although an oversimplification, there are two clear instructions outlined in the Bible that provide a rationale for Christians to engage with others. Firstly is the command from Jesus to his disciples recorded in Matthew 28:19 to 'go and make disciples' (New International Version), an explicit instruction to seek the conversion of non-believers to an active faith in God. This is considered an ongoing task for all believers, as Ellis noted (1990: 89): 'Christians are in the business of passing on to others the content of their faith'.

This agenda can cause considerable concern from those outside the faith who see the purpose of conversion being at odds with the recognised values of informal education (Milson, 1963). To give credence to those concerns, there are some examples of explicit and often insensitive evangelism occurring within an otherwise non-religious youth club setting:

> *At some point in the programme, usually towards the end of the evening, members are gathered together and given a talk about*

some aspect of the Christian faith. To the secular youth worker this appears very strange – a total turn around in the whole ethos of the proceedings.

(Ellis, 1990: 95)

While understandable to Christians looking to share their faith, this kind of approach can be deceptive and dishonest to those participating and has been likened to 'bait and switch' fraud where potential customers are drawn in by a product or service, only to discover that something different is being sold instead (Jolly, 2011). However, an evangelistic approach to Christian youth work is not necessarily incompatible with general youth work principles and there have been attempts to reconcile them. Brierley (2003) proposed that Christian youth ministry should be seen as a specialism within wider youth work practice and argued that where faith-based work adopts general youth work principles it should not be in conflict, even if there is a focus on evangelism.

The second reason that Christians are so active in communities is that there is a clear Biblical mandate that demands Christ-followers engage with other people in acts of service. For those who take their faith seriously it is expected that they will, in varying degrees, sacrifice their own comfort in favour of helping others. While this self-sacrifice is not unique to Christianity, Bible passages such as the parable of The Good Samaritan (Luke 10:30–35), the command to 'love your neighbour as yourself' (Matthew 22:36–40), and the importance of faith being combined with action (James 2:14) all reinforce the issue for believers. This expectation of service, often referred to as 'social action', coupled with a long global tradition of practice is a powerful motivator for Christians to engage in community-focused initiatives beyond the walls of the church.

However despite almost universal acceptance of these two major themes by the various streams of Christianity, there seems to be no consensus on the relationship between them. As Passmore (2004) has put it:

The church has often swung from one pillar to the other, resulting in an emphasis on 'proclamation' at one end of the theological spectrum, and 'social action' at the other

(Passmore, 2004: loc 66)

While much Christian youth work has elements of both these approaches, examples can also be found from one extreme with a sole focus on conversion to the other where faith plays no practical role in what is essentially a humanitarian activity. And there are numerous charitable organisations that once started out as expressions of the Christian faith, but have since become secularised to enable them to more effectively outwork the practical aims of the charity (Todd, 2011: 152). The YMCA is an example of an organisation originally set up for young Christian men, but which opened up its membership and developed effective social programmes instead of purely devotional activities (Binfield, 1973). The potential danger of secularisation for Christian organisations was highlighted by the newly elected Pope Francis I who in his first speech, called on the Catholic Church to retain its religious nature: *If we do not confess to Christ, what would we be? We would end up a compassionate [Non-Government Organisation]* (BBC News, 2013: web).

This statement shows that proclaiming faith is the distinction for Christians. And as we have seen, just like an NGO, Christian youth work does have a purpose or mission. Many of the early Christian youth work pioneers considered themselves missionaries and had at least a partial aim of transmitting the Christian faith to young people (Collins-Mayo et al., 2010: 22). Similarly the social action approach can also be described as 'missional', but rather than conversion through preaching or proclamation, the aim is for transformation through social renewal.

It is important to recognise that despite some emotive language, this is not a hidden or subversive agenda by Christians but a motivating force the same as many other movements and organisations. Just as most charities will have a mission statement and specific aims, much Christian youth work will have a particular focus drawn out of their understanding of God's mission. And where this mission can be explored through dialogue and facilitation, it can be aligned with educative principles (Milson, 1963).

In addition to these two traditional Biblical commands for evangelism and social action, there are also strong emotional motivations for Christian youth work that should not be overlooked. One of these is a deeply personal belief that an individual is destined for a particular work, in this case with young people. This sense of 'calling' or vocation is reasonably common among men and women of faith and is 'often tied to spiritual prompting and the relationship between a person and God' (Doyle, 1999: 29). It has been claimed elsewhere that 'the single most important factor in defining youth work practice rests with the worker' (Jolly 2010: 6) because the nature and character of the individual is of huge significance to the effectiveness of the work. The idea of 'calling' demands a unique commitment and affinity from an individual towards the work, so where someone feels called to the task it often positively spurs their enthusiasm and action. This enthusiasm when combined with personality and ingenuity can be very successful (Henriques, 1933: 60). Of course, this raises many difficult questions about what constitutes being called, and how this can be externally verified due to the lack of evidence or shared enquiry.

Lastly, and importantly, it has been suggested that the hidden agenda of mainstream Christian youth work is 'safety' (Ward, 1996: 184), whereby Christian parents have increasingly wanted to educate and nurture their children in the Christian faith through the 'safe' environment of the church. Certainly most churches provide some form of teaching programme for children and young people that seeks to explain basic tenets of the faith to the younger generation, but a sense of deliberate withdrawal and separation from the wider world can also occur.

The inference from individuals and organisations with this motive is to protect young people from potential unsavoury or destructive moral influences. However it is largely debatable if social separation achieves this purity, particularly when most young people will spend around 30 hours a week in a mixed school environment. As Clark (2001: 80–1) says:

> The church is called less to take care of its own by creating an isolated private community, and more to be a dynamic force of intentional penetration into the adolescent world.

However, Ward argues that this institutional, and often unspoken, agenda to provide Christian teaching and values to young people has also been a significant catalyst in the large growth of employment and training for Christian workers in the UK (Ward 1996: 184).

Each worker or organisation will have a varied mix of these motivations, and others, when approaching work with young people. Unsurprisingly this diversity of motivation has had an impact upon youth work practice and methodology. How an individual or organisation understands the purpose of their work, will dictate the approach they take in practice. A church mainly concerned with the spiritual development of a young person might focus their work on Christian teaching and discipleship, whereas a Christian charity working to support children in poverty might be more concerned with fostering a safe environment through social opportunities. Unfortunately this range of activity is generally referred to as 'youth work', with no further distinction. The only other consistent description for Christian youth work is Youth Ministry.

Youth work and youth ministry

'Youth Ministry' is a common term – particularly popular in the United States – used to describe explicit faith-focused activity aimed at converting and nurturing young Christians. As Collins-Mayo et al. (2010: 24) put it: 'Youth ministry is work with young people who are already part of the Church and incorporates evangelism and discipleship'. Examples of youth ministry include informal Bible study groups for young people; events, festivals and rallies for young Christians; prayer and worship services; and regular social activities for those who attend the church group. Ward (1997: 2) describes this role as more akin to the spiritual tasks of the clergy than of other non-faith youth workers, and so it naturally has a greater emphasis on spiritual development and pastoral care.

As a result, there are strong proponents who believe that youth ministry is, and should remain, distinct from 'secular' youth work. Writers such as Barnett (1951) propose that 'it is a sacred Christian duty to meet the spiritual needs of young people'. Similarly Ashton (1986: 69) states: *Youth work is not Christian if it is not true to Jesus Christ in facing young people with [the] gospel and warning them of the consequences of not accepting it.*

This distinction however highlights the main criticism of Christian youth ministry: that it is controlling and discouraging of independent thought. Sadly it is true that the Christian faith has sometimes been presented as undisputed fact that should be wholly accepted without question, and it is understandable therefore that its proponents have been labelled as 'indoctrinators and brain washers' who seek to restrict autonomy and critical analysis (Pugh 1999: 12–13). However this is not the approach taken by the majority of Christian youth workers who, instead of forcing their beliefs upon others, understand ministry as 'a holy way of living toward God and toward one another' (Dean and Foster 1998: 9). There is also a keen awareness among practitioners that shutting down open discussion provokes young people to think more negatively about Christianity (Kay and Francis 1996) and therefore should be avoided.

Yet even where Christian workers have adopted a more social action approach to their work, aligning with the values of informal education such as choice, conversation, relationships and voluntary participation (Jeffs and Smith, 2005), criticism has been raised that there is no longer any Christian distinction to what they do and it is no different to secular youth work. In fact, Christian youth workers can become so effective at relating to 'non-Christian' young people that those young people's beliefs are validated rather than challenged. In some cases, it has been documented that Christian youth workers are not willing or able to share their own faith despite it being the underlying purpose of the work (Collins-Mayo et al., 2010: 97). Rather, they rely on 'doing good things' and expect young people to ask them 'why?'. Rarely does this happen.

So why are some Christian youth workers not able to convey the passion and motivation for their work? Some are arguing that it's because Christian workers are uncritically accepting the ideology prevalent in much youth work training and adopting a 'strategic liberalism' (Collins-Mayo et al., 2010).

> *Proselytism (or evangelism) of any kind, whether overt or otherwise, is very difficult to justify within this strongly relativist ideological frame-work and so the idea that mature and sympathetic adults can work with young people to share an absolute value-set with them in order to equip them for a fruitful and happy adult life, or to share their faith in such a way that young people might accept it for themselves and benefit from it both temporally and eternally, is consigned to the past and replaced by a strange blend of postmodern relativism and pro-gressive, neo-Marxist, so-called 'liberal' Utopia building.*

(Rephael 2011: web)

This apparent paralysis of workers in articulating their values is surprising given the suggestion that Christian motivation has been examined far more than that of their non-religious counterparts (Pugh 1999). Additionally, all workers should not be value-neutral but show an awareness of their own values and motivations (LSIS 2012: 134).

Unfortunately, this situation leaves Christian youth work between a rock and a hard place. Where workers profess their faith (even if done sensitively) they are criticised for imposing their beliefs, and where they shy away from exploring faith they are criticised for not being overtly Christian.

Some of this identity crisis can be attributed to definition. Even though there is some distinction between youth ministry and youth work, there is still a lot of confusion and the two terms are used interchangeably within Christian environments. It is common for churches to advertise and employ 'youth workers' when they really want a minister – someone to systematically teach the Christian faith to young people within the church congregation. Meanwhile some 'youth ministers' employed by Christian organisations are pioneering excellent informal community-based educative youth work. Both the terms 'ministry' and 'work' are problematic, as they don't adequately describe the diversity of activities undertaken or methodologies behind them. The huge growth in professional training for Christian workers hasn't helped things in this regard. It is possible to do a fully validated JNC course in youth work, or choose one with a ministry/theology module, or do a theology degree with added youth ministry. All these options have a different focus and methodology, yet graduates usually call themselves youth workers.

The domains of Christian youth work

Ward (1997) proposed a basic distinction between Christian youth work and youth ministry. He called the two approaches 'Outside In' and 'Inside Out'. *Outside In* involves working with young people outside of the church community often through an informal education approach that may draw them into church. This way of working is often motivated in part by a desire for social action. *Inside Out* involves ministry with young people already connected to the church around issues of faith and spirituality, with the evangelistic motivation of equipping them to share their faith.

This model has been influential, but it tends to polarise the issue between those who favour one of these ways of working and therefore highlights a classic tension in Christian youth work. It is not uncommon for workers who wish to connect with new young people outside the church (outside in), to be placed in conflict with church leaders who prioritise efforts to engage those within the established church (inside out).

Sadly there are numerous tales of youth ministers and workers who leave churches out of despair that their efforts are misunderstood. The complaint here is that the overall purpose of Christian youth work is too often seen as drawing young people into the established church structures rather than towards God. A great deal of literature in youth ministry assumes this purpose:

> *The church really has no choice, then, but to reach out to this group of people, to bring the gospel to the world of the adolescent, with the ultimate goal of assimilating each child into the greater body of Christ as expressed in the local church*
>
> (Clark, 2001: 80)

But where assimilation is the purpose of the work, it is largely failing. Despite the increase in Christian youth work, there has been growing concern over the state of youth ministry in traditional churches. It has even been suggested that we are seeing a 'generational half life': for every generation that passes, church attendance halves (Voas and Crockett, 2005). This should come as a wakeup call for institutional churches looking to keep their young people safe through providing only insular youth programmes, yet in some cases it has only reinforced the desperate desire to 'hang on' to their young people.

The National Study of Youth and Religion from the USA found that although 3 out of 4 teens in the US say they are 'Christian', they show great ambivalence towards faith. It is suggested that this is because what they have been taught and modelled is a weak and feel-good version of the Christian faith dubbed 'moralistic therapeutic deism' (Smith and Denton 2005). It's a challenge-free Christianity based on being and feeling 'good'. The result is that:

> . . . young people possess no real commitment to or excitement about religious faith. Teenagers tend to approach religious participation, like music and sports, as an extracurricular activity: a good, well rounded thing to do, but unnecessary for an integrated life.

(Dean, 2010: 6)

While the cultural climate in the UK is different to the States, there are similarities in these findings. The term 'almost Christian' will ring true for many Christian youth workers struggling to engage young people in outworking their faith in meaningful ways. Where the purpose of Christian youth work is to integrate the younger generation into church, it is on the whole failing. If it is to present the 'good news' of Christianity in ways that show respect and sensitivity, then it needs to create new forms of community to integrate young believers.

Yet, as we have seen, Christian youth work appears to have grown. Churches are contacting more young people and it may well be that even though youth are missing from more traditional forms of church on a Sunday morning, they are present or connected to other forms of church throughout the week. Short introductory courses on faith, mid-week Bible studies and informal gatherings are all quite common. The reality is that Christian youth work is facing a significant challenge to integrate young people into the wider church congregation.

Stanton (2013) has developed a model of faith-based youth work that draws on Ward's but identifies a middle ground. In the three-domain model there are three 'domains' within Christian youth work that serve a distinct purpose: social provision to meet community needs (Domain 1); smaller faith exploration groups for young people to engage faith on their own terms (Domain 2); and established church services (usually on Sundays) to integrate young people with the established institution (Domain 3).

The three domain model of faith-based youth work

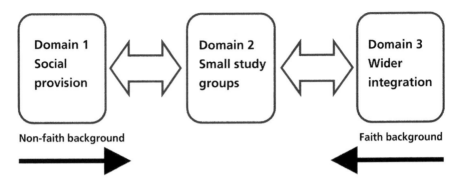

Mirroring Ward's 'Outside In' and 'Inside Out', Stanton shows there are two main directions of travel through the model:

> *Young people from church families usually accessed Christian youth work initially via Domain 3 and young people from outside of the church accessed via Domain 1*

(Stanton, 2013: 200)

The model seems to accurately capture the majority of Christian youth work happening today and is useful in that it allows for a wider spectrum of activity than previous attempts. This includes informal education through social action and faith-based ministry and evangelism (occurring primarily through relationship rather than proclamation). However, just as Ward's model assumed the purpose of youth ministry is to draw young people into established church, the three-domain model also presumes this as one of its purposes through intentional integration into the institutional faith community (Domain 3).

Although this practice of integration does seem to be the norm, there are growing examples of Christian youth work that do not seek to maintain established church structures, and that allow young people to explore faith without the tradition and heritage associated with those institutions. This is based on the understanding that 'the established idea of mission as a bridge into church holds little weight Biblically' (Passmore 2011: 5). So instead, projects such as *Church On The Edge* (COTE) seek to explore 'growing church with young people on the edge as a missionary endeavour and to develop a framework that can facilitate locally grounded and 'resource light', expressions of church' (Passmore 2011: 4). In Ward's language, this approach might be called 'Outside Out' as it looks to engage with those outside of existing church structures and develop an expression of Christian community that remains outside of traditional church.

Developing Christian youth work

There may never be consensus around models and purpose of Christian youth work. Should it have an evangelistic approach, be purely social action or a combination? Should it work to draw young people into existing churches, new expressions of church, or simply have no agenda and seek to support young people where they are at? Whatever the opinion, it does not seem to hinder the wealth of practice that occurs. Yet based on some of the issues described above there is a need for Christian youth work to examine current practice in order to avoid some of the criticism it faces.

First, there is the problem of expectations. It is conceivable that a young person could visit one church youth group and find a thriving activity using an informal education approach and with little faith content. Similarly they could walk into another church youth group and find an academic Bible study using a more formal education approach. Both are valid activities but entirely different, and both are usually simply described as a youth group.

A possible way forward is that where there is some kind of intention in the work, it should be made clear to participants and other stakeholders. Descriptions could be used to help others understand the purpose of the group such as 'faith-based', 'Christian teaching', or simply 'social activities'. If workers can become more up front about their motives, then they can allow young people to make informed choices about what they would like to go to without resorting to the shady practices we explored earlier. It is also true that 'those who have confidence in the gospel have no need to manipulate or coerce young people into accepting the message of Christ' (Brierley, 2003:11).

Stating intention in advance can be of immense benefit to the Christian youth workers who find themselves navigating a complex field of expectations from young people, churches, parents and others. This approach endorses the voluntary principle of youth work. By declaring the nature of the activity, for example through any promotional material, workers are freed from the pressure of managing these various demands and can concentrate on supporting the young people in their care. In this way, the messages presented by Christian youth workers can become more coherent as they will be relevant to the audience in attendance.

We need to identify what it is we wish to communicate and then look for those activities and experiences that put the message across.

(Ellis, 1990: 98)

Second, there are questions around how Christian youth work relates to non-faith or secular work. We have examined the large amount of cross-over between youth work and youth ministry, with the two terms used interchangeably with much confusion. In reality, it is probably useful to recognise that Christian youth work and youth ministry are multifaceted:

. . . it is about facilitating and empowering young people to have the better, fuller, more abundant, rich and satisfying life . . . This involves being concerned about their whole lives, not just the faith bit, wanting to see them fulfil their potential and be all God created them to be.

(Nash, 2011: loc 341)

Sometimes the ideological agenda in Christian work can move outside of accepted youth work values. This is understandable given the beliefs of Christians and the mission of the church, but the danger is in labelling it all as generic youth work. Christians need to become more selective, and more understanding in how they describe their work. In some instances it aligns perfectly with general youth work values, at other times it falls outside of what is usually considered youth work.

Last, there is also a case for allowing more dialogue between workers of faith and secular beliefs. A better understanding would undoubtedly help allay any fears or suspicions of the other's agenda, lead to better collaboration, and ultimately enable better support for young people.

Overall, there is usually a clear rationale for Christian youth work that falls within general youth work principles. Despite some concerns, the Christian community does a vast amount of positive work for and with young people. And as is the case with all youth work, the important factor is that 'regardless of position and settings, Christian workers must be a person of integrity' (Nash and Hirst, 2011: 3).

References

Ashton, M. (1986) *Christian Youth Work*. Eastbourne: Kingsway Publications.
Atkinson-Small, J. (2012, July 13). *Youth Clubs are Thriving Thanks to Volunteers. Is this the 'Big Society' in Action?* Retrieved March 15, 2013 from Mail Online: http://www.dailymail.co.uk/debate/article-2173022/Youth-clubs-thriving-thanks-volunteers-Is-Big-Society-action.html
Barnett. (1951) *The Church Youth Club*. London: Epworth Press.

BBC News. (2013 March 14) *'Pope Francis Warns Church Could Become "Compassionate NGO".'* Retrieved March 15, 2013 from BBC News: http://www.bbc.co.uk/news/world-europe-21793224.

Binfield, C. (1973) *George Williams and the YMCA*. London: Heinemann.

Brierley, D. (2003) *Joined Up: An Introduction To Youth Work and Ministry*. Carlisle: Authentic Lifestyle.

Brierley, P. (2000) *The Tide is Running Out: What the English Church Attendance Survey Reveals*. London: Christian Research.

Buttery, S., and Telling, M. (2009) *More Than Sundays*. Moggerhanger: Family Matters Institute.

Children & Young People Now. (2011, June 14). *Youth Groups Find Alternative Funding to Make up for Government Spending Cuts*. Retrieved March 15, 2013 from Children & Young People Now: http://www.cypnow.co.uk/go/youth_work/article/1074694/youth-groups-find-alternative-funding-government-spending-cuts/

Clark, C. (2001) The Missional Approach to Youth Ministry. In Senter, M. H. III (Ed.) *For Views of Youth Ministry and the Church: Inclusive Congregational, Preparatory, Missional, Strategic*. (ePub ed.) El Cajon: Youth Specialties.

Collins-Mayo, S., Mayo, B., and Nash, S. (2010) *The Faith of Generation Y*. London: Church House Publishing.

Davies, B. (2010) What do we Mean by Youth Work? In Batsleer, J. and Davies, B. (Eds.) *What is Youth Work? Empowering Youth and Community Work Practice*. Exeter: Learning Matters.

Dean, K. C. (2010) *Almost Christian: What the Faith of Our Teenagers is Telling the American Church*. New York: Oxford University Press.

Dean, K. C., and Foster, R. (1998) *The Godbearing Life. The Art of Soul Tending for Youth Ministry*. Nashville: Upper Room Books.

Doyle, M. E. (1999) Called to be an Informal Educator. *Youth and Policy*, 65, 28–37.

Eagar, W. M. (1953) *Making Men. A history of Boys Clubs and Related Movements*. London: University of London Press.

Ellis, J. W. (1990) Informal Education – A Christian Perspective. In Jeffs, T. and Smith, M. (Eds.) *Using Informal Education*. Buckingham: Open University Press.

Green, M. (1999) Editorial. *Youth and Policy*, 65, 1–7.

Henriques, B. (1933) *Club Leadership*. London: Oxford University Press.

HMSO. (1960) *The Youth Service in England and Wales*. London: HMSO.

Jeffs, T. and Smith, M. K. (2005) *Informal Education. Conversation, Democracy and Learning*. Nottingham: Educational Heretics Press.

Jolly, J. (2010) Local Youth Work. In Smith, M. and Rogers, A. (Eds.) *Journeying Together*. Lyme Regis: Russell House.

Jolly, J. (2011, November) Unashamed Youth Ministry. *Youthwork Magazine*.

Kay, W. and Francis, L. J. (1996) *Drift from the Churches: Attitudes Toward Christianity During Childhood and Adolescence*. Cardiff: University of Wales Press.

LSIS. (2012) *Youth Work National Occupational Standards*. London: LSIS.

Milson, F. W. (1963) *Social Group Method and Christian Education*. London: Chester House Publications.

Nash, P. and Hirst, S. (2011) Politician of Integrity. In Nash, S. (Ed.) *Youth Ministry: A Multifaceted Approach*. London: Society for the Promotion of Christian Knowledge (SPCK).

Nash, S. (2011) Introduction. In Nash, S. (Ed.) *Youth Ministry A Multi-Faceted Approach* (Kindle ed.). London: Society for Promoting of Christian Knowledge (SPCK).

Passmore, R. (2004) *Meet Them Where They're At* (Kindle ed.).

Passmore, R. (2011) *Reconnected: Releasing the Imagination Around Mission and Church in a Post Modern World*. Exeter: University of Exeter.

Pew Research. (2011) *Global Christianity – A Report on the Size and Distribution of the World's Christian Population*. Washington: Pew Research Center.

Pugh, C. (1999) Christian Youth Work: Evangelism or Social Action? *Youth and Policy*, 65, 8–27.

Rephael, J. W. (2011, March 24) *Youth Work, Ideology and Faith*. Retrieved September 09, 2013 from ὅτι ἐστι – intellectual honestly: http://rephael.wordpress.com/2011/03/24/ideological-youthwork/

Smith, C. and Denton, M. (2005) *Soul Searching: The Religious and Spiritual Lives of American Teenagers*. New York: Oxford University Press.

Smith, M. (1988) *Developing Youth Work, Informal Education, Mutal Aid and Popular Practice*. Milton Keynes: Open University Press.

Smith, M. (1999) *Youth Work: An Introduction*. Retrieved March 15, 2012 from the encyclopedia of informal education: www.infed.org/youthwork/b-yw.htm.

Stanton, N. (2013) Faith-based Youth Work – Lessons From the Christian Sector. In Curran, S., Harrison, R. and MacKinnon, D. (Eds.) *Working with Young People* (2nd ed.). London: Sage.

Todd, S. C. (2011) *Fast Living. How the Church Will End Extreme Poverty*. Colorado Springs: Compassion International.

Voas, D. and Crockett, A. (2005) Religion in Britain: Neither Believing nor Belonging. *Sociology*, 39, 11–28.

Ward, P. (1996) *Growing Up Evangelical: Youth Work and the Making of a Subculture*. London: Society for Promoting Christian Knowledge (SPCK).

Ward, P. (1997) *Youthwork and the Mission of God*. London: Society for the Promotion of Christian Knowledge (SPCK).

CHAPTER 4

The Voices of Young British Muslims: Identity, Belonging and Citizenship

Sughra Ahmed

People challenge British Muslims that you're either British or Muslim; why can't we be both?

Much is written about young British Muslims, but what are young Muslims themselves saying and thinking about the lives they live? *Seen and Not Heard: Voices of Young British Muslims** brought together the views – the thoughts, aspirations, and frustrations – held by young British Muslims of over 15 different ethnicities, from across England, Scotland and Wales. It enabled female and male voices to express, in their own words, their out-look and how they feel they are perceived. With over half of British Muslims under the age of 25, the findings contained within the research provide an insight into some of the more pertinent questions asked by policy makers, statutory services and community institutions concerning a growing genera-tion positioned to make their impact on British society. This chapter explores the notions of identity, citizenship and belonging in the lives of young British Muslims, drawing on findings from the *Seen and Not Heard* research. It goes on to indicate some implications for youth work with young Muslims, based on these findings.

Since 9/11, and to some extent since the events surrounding the controver-sial publication in 1988 of *Satanic Verses* by Salman Rushdie, debates about

---

* This chapter was originally in the report *Seen and Not Heard: Voices of Young British Muslims* by Sughra Ahmed. It was published by the Policy Research Centre, based at the Islamic Foundation. The Centre specialises in research, policy, advice and training on issues related to British Muslims. It brings together policy, academic and community expertise to inform and shape current policy thinking. It seeks to enhance the policy responses to some of the critical issues being debated today around identity, citizenship, security and the lives of Muslim citizens.

Britain's Muslims have occurred across popular and political spectrums alike, on such topics as loyalty, belonging, citizenship and identity. Feelings of allegiance and faithfulness are complex notions to grasp; contemporary debates link these to discussions on how we identify when an individual has a sense of belonging to a community and understands their rights and responsibilities as a member of that community. Such questions are often asked of those who may be considered to be recent arrivals, migrant communities and, since 9/11, young British Muslims. Young people, regardless of background, are often at a stage where they are trying to understand their place in the world and, when faced with complexities around identity, belonging and citizenship, find it problematic that they are being asked to define who they are to the wider British communities they are part of. Often those who ask such questions have a perceived identity of young British Muslims, which is formed of preconceived ideas and, at times, typecasting and, indeed, racism.

As well as facing questions and challenges to their loyalty, young Muslims today, in common with others, are living in unprecedented times both in terms of globalisation and the popularity of new media. They are also facing complex concepts such as being pressed to define their identity in the light of national and international events that are instantaneously transported across the globe, pushing young Muslims to provide explanations and answers for the actions of others. The burden of proof that Islam is a peaceful religion and that Muslims are law-abiding citizens is often placed at the door of young British Muslims. Not only will this often fail to provide conclusive answers, it is also unfair. This process is especially damaging when myths and stereotypes surmount accurate information and result in young British Muslims being portrayed as a threat to the wellbeing of the wider British society.

Questions about identity, belonging and citizenship are closely related and often overlap in discussions with young people. In such dialogue examples of other societies are often referred to, particularly those of Bosnia and migration within and beyond the Indian subcontinent; for example; first-hand experience from elders:

> From Professor Anwar's paper, we see that 60% of Muslims in Britain were born here and they now represent the second and third generations. I am from the remaining 40%. But I was born a British subject in India where it became unsafe for me and my parents to reside so we sought sanctuary in the then East Pakistan. We learned the language, the customs and the culture but eventually we were told that we were not loyal and so we had to leave. We made our way to England

nineteen years ago. Now again I am asked 'are you loyal and do you belong to this country?'

(Seddon et al., 2003: 104)

Many young Muslims feel comfortable with their British identity and are confused as to why questions about citizenship are circuiting British society. Some feel that loyalty to a country springs from their religious values. They recognise that their faith strongly encourages allegiance to the nation state so they are governed by the law of the land and are answerable for their actions in the same way as their non-Muslim counterparts. Some have argued that loyalty is derived from feeling involved in the shaping of national identity as opposed to living in a climate of an excluding nationalism which most may reject (Seddon et al., 2003). Throughout his research for *Made in Bradford*, Alam (2006: 16) noticed '. . . that yet again, here was a group or type of individuals being talked about, not being talked to. Alongside this absence of real communication, a demonisation of this "type", and indeed a wider ethnic group, was continuing to develop'.

The complexity of the debate includes identities and histories, both pre and post migration. It is further complicated by the focus of the media and other agencies on attaching labels, implying Muslims are foreign beings within our borders and becoming obsessed with young Muslims and their views on international affairs. Young Muslims often feel confused when their British identity is questioned in public domains. The way in which some Muslim communities and individuals (especially young and male) are portrayed suggests that a construction of an alien, or at best an insular and distinct, culture is taking root. Alam (2006: 20) explains that 'Now, more than ever, British Muslims are asked to prove themselves as not only loyal and peaceful, but also as integrated citizens.' Major changes in policy and political outlook coupled with dramatic global events mean that British Muslims today find themselves in the midst of interconnected debates touching on immigration and nationalism as well as citizenship and integration. However, the 'miniaturisation of people' (a reduction of the complexities involved in understanding and appreciating a community) potentially has a long-term effect because it ignores the 'intricacies . . . and multiple loyalties' of plural groups such as the multicultural British Muslim community (Sen, 2006: 20).

Identity formation is influenced by many factors as young people grow from childhood into adolescence and beyond. This process is exacerbated by the essentialisation of youth today. Often young people, of whatever background, can be seen as delinquent groups that don't contribute positively to society and undermine the safety of people around them. This process does not recognise colour, religion, and creed; instead it feeds on stereotypes of 'hoodies', gangs, ASBOs and 'yobs', which are often generalised to all young people across the UK. The creation of subcultures is particularly common amongst young people. According to Brake (1990), subcultures are not created as the antithesis of wider culture or in opposition, but instead, as argued by Murdock and McCron (1976), they are an expression and extension of the dominant meaning system. These subcultures are not usually deviant; they rarely become a counterculture (Brake, 1990).

Young British Muslims often share a particular subculture through attending a Madrasa system with their peers. For around two hours per day, Monday to Friday, many young Muslims aged between five and thirteen years attend a supplementary school to gain a rudimentary knowledge of Islam. This learning often involves concepts such as prayer and worship as well as learning to read the Qur'an by rote. This process, which lasts several years, plays a part in the way in which young Muslims learn to understand their faith and their own relationship with it. The experience of attending a Madrasa can be challenging for young people in that they tend to go from an environment at school where they are encouraged to ask questions and take a keen interest in learning, either academically or through play, to the Mosque space where learning is demonstrated through memorisation alone, and where having questions is understood by many teachers as being culturally disrespectful. Without consciously realising it, young British Muslims learn from an early age to negotiate these two worlds. This 'schizophrenic' lifestyle continues from their early years all the way through to adolescence and beyond, negotiating two different realities: one outside the home and their faith/cultural community and the other within it.

The research

The research methodology, which closely informs this chapter, includes the following:

- Nine focus groups with young British Muslims conducted in Glasgow, Bradford, Manchester, Leicester, Birmingham, Cardiff, Tower Hamlets in East London, Brixton in South London and Slough.
- Nine interviews with youth workers and young people from Muslim, Christian, Jewish and state settings who are working to support their local communities.

• Secondary research including a literature review exploring existing material that has been published in this area.

This chapter draws upon the focus groups with young Muslims. Muslim communities are distributed around the country; they are not homogenous and can often be divided along ethnic and other lines. Therefore it was important for the research to hear from as many ethnic heritages as possible. All of those who participated had lived all or most of their lives in the localities in which they were interviewed.

Influence, engagement and tradition

Peers were cited by the young Muslims as having the greatest influence on their lives and identities; the desire to be accepted by others like them overrides other influences:

> I'm saying a person is mainly influenced by his friends because does he spend more time with his family or at school? . . . He is going to be at school with his friends for 6 hours of the day, 5 days a week, he's away from his family. Saturday, Sunday, he wakes up, comes down, has breakfast, he's gonna go back to his friends again, so most of the week he's with his mates. Whatever his mates are gonna do, he's gonna be doing the same thing, so if they're all smoking pot in the corner, he's gonna be smoking.

This influence is not necessarily negative. If peers were involved in learning or employment, it acted as an influencing factor on other young Muslims who aspired to be like their closest friends, subconsciously taking them to be their mentors.

Young Muslims explained that they feel engaged in and part of society. There was an overarching sense of a need to engage: this was a common sentiment in the groups and appeared to be borne out of a need to respond to contemporary issues. Muslim young people are often more politically literate and aware of global issues than their peers because recent events have forced them to be. Therefore Muslim youth are not choosing to remove themselves from the mainstream democratic system but the system can be unwilling or unable to listen to their views of 'dissent', deciding to label these as disloyal. Muslim young people are not alone in feeling they are unheard but, worryingly, may be the primary group scrutinised for how they respond to such feelings of alienation.

Young Muslim women in the Brixton group, predominantly of African-Caribbean background, felt they were among the most engaged members of the wider communities in which they lived, even when they compared themselves to Muslim communities in other areas of the country. This sense of wider engagement was strongly expressed by these young women who customarily wore plain black coverings, over their faces in most cases (often labelled as a sign of disengagement by media and political discourses). A key basis for their view of themselves as engaged was a lack of cultural baggage, which they felt held back other more typical (Asian) Muslim communities, who they perceived to be culturally entrenched rather than religiously conscious. These young women viewed a strong adherence to an ethnic (usually Asian) culture as an obstacle to integration.

Young Muslims in Scotland argued for a return to tradition. Young people in our study reflected on ideas such as arranged marriage, respect for parents and other 'traditional' values, which play a strong role in many Muslim families. It was somewhat surprising to hear that arranged marriages were now being sought by some of the young people, who were turning to their parents and asking them to arrange their marriage – often abroad. When probed further, the young people expressed that they had seen many such marriages work and keeping their parents happy was a key factor in their own happiness; therefore arranged marriages were seen as a positive choice rather than an act of oppression or compulsion. Of course, this differs from a situation where the young people involved do not wish to marry the person of their parents' choice (forced marriage), but in this scenario it was the young people who were actively pursuing such lines. These young people have seen a generation before them wait longer than was traditionally the norm to settle down into married life, an increasing number of people having difficulty finding a suitable partner, as well as having observed breakdown in families.

This viewpoint presents a stark contrast with the female participants of the Tower Hamlets focus group where young women vocalised how difficult their parents' cultural traditions had become for them as young British Muslims. They explained that they had 'been economical with the truth' to their parents about their social lives outside of the home because any mixed gender activity was disapproved of. They also indicated they would go against their parents' wishes when the subject of marriage arises; should their parents wish for them to marry abroad through an arranged marriage, they would do everything they could to dissuade them.

In Brixton, the picture of a religious group connected through their faith and positive local experiences was echoed by the male participants. The young people's positive experiences depended on them having a space within which they could live an ideal of a 'true' Muslim life without negative intrusion. Any negative intrusions would impinge on their understanding of their identity as young Muslims from Brixton, the majority of whom came from a convert (or as they termed, revert) community. Their views tended to be more conservative than in the other focus groups. Their conviction of the idea that they are practising young Muslims and engaged within British – or at the very least, Brixton – society, was balanced by the belief that, should anything hamper their way of life and render them unable to live in this way, then migration to a 'Muslim' country would be an option:

> [As] Muslims we are supposed to migrate to a place where it is Islamic and this country is not an Islamic country.

The young person expressed this opinion on the basis of a particular understanding of Islam:

> So yeah, the reason why . . . obviously because we believe we are supposed to be in a Muslim country that's what makes us feel like . . . you know, technically we are not supposed to be here. We should be in a Muslim climate but we were born here.

Engagement in this sense, then, was equated with feeling 'comfortable' rather than through civic representation. A sense of agitation was, in some cases, expressed that, 'No one is trying to get to know us', that on sight of the black veil, people 'automatically assume you can't speak English' and, when pressed, that 'exceptions are made for other people'.

According to these Brixton participants, society called for Muslims to concede some religious teachings and the vast majority of Muslim bodies had done just that. The young people were convinced that government funding for local projects, including for the Prevention of Violent Extremism, required a compromise of fundamentals. They complained of the violation of fundamentals in social aspects pointing, for example, to the 'mixing' of males and females. One participant asserted that inquisitive young minds fell into two camps: those who fell for the compromises, and those who were agitated by them and their claim to represent Islam. In the latter view, the 'liberal' or 'sell-out' Islam being promulgated by the Muslim media and some Muslim organisations was viewed as doing a disservice to young Muslims in that they are now faced with two extreme choices:

1. The Extremists: young people from Brixton felt characters such as Abu Hamza and Abu Qatada were given far too much time and space in the media, which contributes to radicalisation, especially in institutions such as prisons.

> *A lot of the extremism comes from non-Muslim media outlets as well. I mean they might see a Bin Laden video or Abu Qatada speech on the BBC of all places and say that we are trying to combat extremism and the Muslim community is not doing more to help and they are making the problem ten times worse by giving these people a platform to speak on. Do you know what I mean?*

Things become even more challenging when young people look for an alternative to the likes of such extremists, and in this case, young men felt:

> *There is no organisation representing the youth. What they are doing in authority in most of the cases, they are chasing the youth away so that Abu Hamza comes and says 'look, they are trying to dumb down Islam'.*

2. The Sell-Outs: the second extreme was identified as the 'sell-outs' who were seen as representing large groups within the British Muslim community but as compromising on key issues which the young people of Brixton felt were at the heart of Islam such as dress, music and shaking hands with the opposite gender.

Such extremes were perceived to be unrepresentative of a true practice of Islam. Therefore the young people either felt disillusioned with authority and representation or confused as to why it is these two extremes that represent Islam in the public domain. The notion arising here is that there is no organisation that genuinely works for young Muslims; however much this may be contested, this perception indicates that there are important fractures in Muslim communities that have not been bridged. This view is also compounded by a sense of personal inner turmoil in feeling rejected by society:

> *I was born in this country and I have rights, I obey the law yeah and why should I be made to feel like this really, you know I'm an outcast, I did something wrong because I am a Muslim?*

An experience shared by a young man from Glasgow reflected upon the parochial perception of young Muslims:

There were some kind of roadworks and there was this old woman . . . walking towards . . . she started walking faster . . . and as soon as she walks past us she goes, 'This is my country, not yours.' We stood there and we waited for her to go past. Now really, us, we were in school back then, so if it was someone younger, I'm not going to deny we would have probably started . . . but it was an old woman. What could we say to her? . . . It wasn't because I didn't have anything to say; I can have a mouth on me when I want, but if I did start saying something to her then, the rest of the white people walking up and down that street would have thought, 'Young Muslim mob attacking an old woman.' It would have been on the headlines and everything!

Young Muslims often view public perceptions of them as negative, challenging and difficult.

Foreign policy and sense of belonging

In Slough, there were marked differences in what the participants believed was the agenda behind the 'war on terror'. In a clear disagreement between two participants, a case was made for the 'war on terror' being a war directly on Islam, against the case of a war dealing with a problem that they as Muslims did not subscribe to. Both participants felt they represented the majority view of British Muslim youth, though they recognised the subjective nature of their positions. The holder of the former opinion felt a strong sense of connectivity and allegiance to Muslims overseas, in preference to Muslim and non-Muslim British citizens. This preference, according to the claimant, was embedded within the teachings of the Muslim scripture (the Qur'an), and was, for the participant, not an area of negotiation. Although the use of terrorism was not condoned, the cause of such acts and the blame was squarely put down to historic and contemporary issues of modern foreign policy. One participant added that, in the search for identity and belonging, 'had it not been for pro-integration groups such as the Islamic Society of Britain, I could have been attracted to the easier [more absolute] message of an extremist group.'

Debates about loyalty were driven by ongoing war (for example, in Iraq), where a sense of national belonging was acknowledged but affected by concerns overseas. Despite their sense of a local connection, a sense of national belonging was hardest to ascertain in the views of participants in Brixton. There was also a closer affiliation with people outside Britain among the Brixton young people. One participant argued there was nothing 'holding' her in Britain, and so she felt 'no connection'. This was a measure in her mind of the cultural norms and religious beliefs of mainstream Britain, and its distance from the notion of Islamic religion (influenced by Saudi religious thought). Participants often spoke in terms of 'them and us' in regards to their relationship with non-Muslims, even though they were often unaware of this until probed further.

Identity and belonging: false 'choices'

As with many other young people, young Muslims experienced tension when it came to questions of national identity, particularly those living in England. By contrast, their Scottish and Welsh counterparts felt a strong sense of identity in being Scottish and Welsh and, when questioned further, they reluctantly disclosed a sense of Britishness, but their affinities lay with Scotland and Wales. A very small number of young Muslims confidently expressed their Englishness and in fact became confused by the question of identity: 'Why am I being asked such obvious questions?' When the researcher explained that identity and loyalty were topical issues that the wider British public was trying to understand, the young people explained they had only ever known England and understood themselves to be English and British.

Despite the young Scottish Muslims feeling determinedly Scottish, this became problematic when we discussed how they are perceived by other Scots. It was generally agreed that the majority of Scots would not understand Muslims to be Scottish. However, in one scenario where a young man did feel others saw him as Scottish, it had a strong impact on his understanding of himself:

> Scotland beat Italy, and the day of the match I was in town, and that day was the first day I ever felt properly Scottish. I think there were four or five white people drunk out of their nut and I was on the train, and one actually came up to me and he put his arm around me . . . and said, 'Do you know what guy? You better be supporting Scotland today.' I said, 'Of course I am.' He said, 'I'm going to buy you a flag.' I said, 'Why?' and he said, 'Because you're Scottish too.' And that's the first time I've ever felt properly Scottish.

The group in Cardiff, by contrast, had far fewer tensions in accepting a sense of belonging. They were British, and felt it:

I feel, genuinely, we do try our best to engage . . . from being brought up in Cardiff . . . I do think, yeah, most Muslims from what I see . . . do try to engage.

I went and studied in [nearby] Swansea and there was a distinct [difference], you know, they were completely segregated, it was like their own community, as Muslims . . . they were segregated from the non-Muslim community, even, I suppose, there was a distinction between the old and the young.

The presence of a 'with it' mosque Imam, who was instrumental in creating an inclusive and relaxed atmosphere at a popular, local mosque and its community youth centre, had clearly helped the Cardiff young people adjust and negotiate their multiple identities. Almost all young people in this group said they would use their Imam as their most trusted port of call for religious questions. Female participants mentioned they would ask the Imam's wife in the first instance. When asked why they did not go directly to the Imam, they responded that they could if they wanted to, but usually asked his wife. A notable feature of the Cardiff group was the blend of ethnicities. The ethnic diversity meant the chief language of communication was English which enabled greater communication between the Imam and young people. The participants in Cardiff were acutely aware that their environment was not typical of most Muslim communities in the UK, and clearly valued the local Imam. They referred to nearby Swansea as a place that was not as lucky, and alluded to socio-economic challenges:

The valleys has a lot of socio-economic problems and I think that has quite a lot of influence on the way that non-Muslims perceive Muslims and the way that Muslims interact with non-Muslims, and I think it's mainly due to the poverty and that kind of thing; I don't think you can underestimate the impact that that kind of thing can have . . .

However, as with participants in Brixton, there was a strong local sense of independence with little real connection to or experience of other locations. How they viewed other Muslim communities was, ironically, based largely on portrayals in the media.

In other parts of the country, young Muslims argued that being British and feeling integrated was different for them than for their white counterparts. The young people explained that, for them, feeling part of British culture meant a feeling of engagement whether through employment; education for those at college or university; or the social activities they were involved in such as campaigning for the environment, for animal welfare and poorer communities. They explained, that even though they may not be as interested in what are often deemed to be aspects of 'youth culture' (e.g. clubbing, drinking), they still have a strong sense of Britishness and integration. As one young man in Slough made clear:

> When I go to school for example, I wouldn't do the things that a lot of them are doing, like drinking, going out. These sorts of things aren't really typical of a young Muslim to do, be it because of religious reasons or our families or the culture that we come from. Whatever the reason is, we aren't really engaged at that sort of level so I guess you could say detached from that sense . . . But we're involved in other levels, I think that it's really broad, you can't just paint everyone with the same brush really . . .

Other sorts of belonging: class and political action

There appeared to be a class consciousness in the minds of the young Muslim participants; they came largely from deprived areas and were clearly aware of their working-class identity. When discussing community involvement in maintaining good neighbourhoods, getting involved in causes which affect the whole of society, some felt this was where the responsibility of the more affluent Muslim community lay:

> How many Muslims, it's not even us, like if you think about Muslims who call themselves a certain class or whatever – how many of those take part in issues like the environment, Greenpeace and animal rights and stuff?

Although they desired to make a change in the world, some couldn't envisage making that difference directly themselves; they saw such causes as outside their sphere of influence. Those who did participate in such causes did so through established organisations which work within communities. Through such vehicles, some of the young people had been able to become more involved, which increased their sense of social responsibility and awareness of both the issues they were campaigning for and an awareness of themselves. The roles they played enabled them to understand their own likes and dislikes better as well as discovering where their skills and talents lay.

Frank and open discussions

The challenges young Muslims face often require frank and open discussions on topics that may be controversial and possibly sensitive. Cultural taboos often inhibit such discussions and force young Muslims to either repress their experiences and concerns or speak with peers who are ill equipped to deal with the challenges. Research by the Muslim Youth Helpline* (MYH) highlighted the top five areas around which their clients seek support. These were 'relationships'; 'mental health'; 'religion'; 'offending and rehabilitation'; and 'sexuality and sexual health' (Malik et al., 2007: 26). Although MYH statistics show that 58% of their clients are from London, they are becoming increasingly known and trusted in other parts of England; 26% of their client enquiries are from the northwest of England, despite having no physical presence there and their advertising being London-centric. This is a strong message from the young people in the northwest region – a reflection of their needs and the desire to contact those whom they perceive best served to deal with the issues, in this case not their local authorities, or local community groups, but a Muslim helpline based in London.

Young people in the focus groups discussed the challenges they face in finding support for resolving personal concerns in their localities. For example, they did not feel they could approach their parents to discuss relationships issues because of the religious and cultural barriers they felt exist between parents and their children:

> *For something like that you wouldn't talk to your parents because, alright, at the end of the day they are your parents but it's that respect at the end of the day.*

> *I feel awkward going home and saying, mum this happened today with this girl I met, whatever, you'd feel awful wouldn't you . . .*

Although respect, religion and culture were the key reasons why young Muslims would not look to their parents for discussions on some of the topics that concern them, they also highlighted an added dimension that prevents them from fully engaging with their elders, the intergenerational gap:

---

* The Muslim Youth Helpline is a registered charity that provides pioneering faith and culturally sensitive services to Muslim youth across the UK. Its core service is a free and confidential counseling service available nationally via telephone, e-mail, online and a face-to-face befriending service in the Greater London area. The service uses male and female volunteers trained in specialized support skills to respond to client enquiries.

I think 'cos with the generation gaps a lot of parents have actually come from abroad . . . are actually still traditional ways, some of them haven't learnt the language for example so what usually happens is sons and daughters who have virtually now grown up in the English society have now taken over . . . so the parents leave it to them to make their decisions . . .

The young men argued that there is a visible gender imbalance in treatment from parents, which means boys and girls in the same household are treated differently to such a degree that it affects their life chances. Interestingly, the young Pakistani-British men were the loudest in voicing these concerns:

The Muslims, the majority of the Muslims in Bradford are Asian right, Pakistani, they don't give girls the chance. That's what I think. They don't give girls the chance as much as they give the guys to go out and take part.

The research shows that discourses on identity, loyalty and belonging are varied across the country and across Muslim communities. While the expected issues of tension such as foreign policy (and government policy more broadly), being treated in a hostile way and aspects of social life such as 'pub culture' did arise; the vast majority of young people that spoke to us felt no contradiction between their religious and national identities. They felt part of British society and wanted to be treated as equals, not to be privileged, nor discriminated against. This negotiated aspect of their identity and how they locate themselves in society also came across as something that is in creative flux – it is constantly being re-defined in light of politics, access to global and new media and the influence of peers and community.

Conclusion and implications for youth work

Questions about loyalty often centre on the identity, sense of belonging and citizenship of young British Muslims. Debates on such concepts often neglect the complexities young British Muslims face in terms of their feeling British while others perceive them as foreigners. Many of the young Muslims in this study argued that their loyalty and belonging lie in the United Kingdom. Alongside this loyalty came a sense of citizenship in which they were aware of their rights and responsibilities as British subjects. However, the young Muslims faced questions that imply a choice between their religion and nationality needs to be made and the popular perception is that the two are juxtaposed against one another. Young British Muslims commented that, for them, the two do not contradict one another.

However, on a cultural level, Muslims of the second generation sometimes felt pulled between two cultures; and some decided that they would adopt a British Muslim culture while rejecting that of their parents. Other young Muslims may now be more comfortable in negotiating new identities and the heritage of their parents and grandparents, and we may thus see a partial return to some aspects of traditional culture. For example, arranged marriages were discussed, with parental involvement, mutual consent and a genuine desire to find marriage partners through networks and extended families of parents or elders and friends.

Youth work with young British Muslims needs to take account of these complexities by providing safe spaces for open discussion and peer-to-peer learning. The focus groups for this research demonstrated that young people felt a sense of confidence and assurance when given the space to discuss and share experiences with their peers. These conversations can strengthen young people's self-esteem, a crucial factor in the process of forming their identities and negotiating their way in the world. In addition, an intergenerational learning experience would serve to both enhance the relationship between first and second/third generations of Muslims as well as inspiring a greater sense of being stakeholders amongst young Muslims. Learning about the investment their elders made during key historic events such as WWI and WWII, economic migration and the process of integration will help to pass on the rich history of first generation Muslims and create a stronger sense of rootedness amongst the younger generations across the UK today.

References

Alam, M.Y. (2006) *Made in Bradford*. Pontefract: Route Publishing.

Brake, M. (1990) *Comparative Youth Culture: The Sociology of Youth Cultures and Youth Subcultures in America, Britain and Canada*. London: Routledge.

Husain, M.G. (2004) *Muslim Youth and Madrasa Education*. New Delhi: Institute of Objective Studies.

Malik, R., Shaikh, A. and Suleyman, M. (2007) *Providing Faith and Culturally Sensitive Support Services to Young British Muslims*. Leicester: National Youth Agency.

Murdock, G. and McCron, R. (1976) Consciousness of Class and Consciousness of Generation. In Hall, S. and Jefferson, T. (Eds.) *Resistance Through Rituals*. London: Hutchinson.

Seddon, M., Hussain, D. and Malik, N. (2003) *British Muslims: Loyalty and Belonging*. Leicester: The Islamic Foundation.

Sen, A. (2006) *Identity and Violence: The Illusion of Destiny*. London: Penguin.

CHAPTER 5

Faith-based Youth Work and Civil Society

Nigel Pimlott

This chapter considers the relationship between faith-based youth work, citizenship and civil society. It does so with reference to recent and historical policy initiatives, influential concepts and ideological challenges.

Background

The twenty-first century has given birth to a number of policy initiatives that have endeavoured to build civil society and develop a sense of citizenship in young people. The nature and precise detail of these has varied over time but, irrespective of which political party has been in power, there has been a desire to encourage young people to develop their sense of citizenship as part of a strong civil society. These initiatives have included a range of policies designed to re-shape youth provision such as *Transforming Youth Work* (DfEE, 2001) and *Positive for Youth* (DfE, 2011a) as well as broader, almost philosophical, concepts such as 'Respect' (Respect Task Force, 2006) and the 'Big Society' (Cameron, 2009).

Recent times have also witnessed some renaissance in the provision of faith-based youth work as many faith bodies have entered or re-entered the fields of social action, educational provision and ministry work with young people. Academic courses have produced a new generation of faith-based workers qualified from Level 2 through to postgraduate. Given the history of the UK, it is perhaps not surprising that the Christian faith constituency has been pre-eminent, but emerging evidence from my own academic research indicates similar trends in other faiths (Pimlott, 2011).

However, the extent to which this renaissance is being taken seriously by policy-makers is unclear. If faith-based groups are to play a key partnership role in developing civil society then some suspicions need to be overcome. These include the belief that government is simply using faith groups to: deliver government agendas via the back door; supply their own resources on behalf of the state; do things on the cheap and engage with diverse and hard-to-reach communities without truly valuing the contribution faith makes to society.

Agreed definitions about what is meant by faith-based youth work are contested and interpretations vary from faith to faith. There is a need to avoid Christian-centric definitions as these do little to promote inclusive approaches that are worthy of representing 'faith-based youth work' as a field and community of practice. Indeed, there is some faith-based work with young people that does not coincide with broadly accepted understandings of appropriate youth work practice. For example, some organisations, in the name of faith, have a propensity, or at least a perceived propensity, to manipulate young people or act from extreme fundamentalist principles that can translate into prejudice and hate – issues given further consideration by Green (2010: 123– 38). Notwithstanding these complexities; for simplicity, this chapter treats any work undertaken with young people by people of faith, when those people are explicitly acting in the name of their faith, as 'faith-based youth work'.

In a similar vein, definitions about what is meant by 'citizenship' are also problematic. As Cooper (in Fitzsimons et al., 2011: 129) suggests, how citizenship is defined in mainstream policy terms determines 'who is in' and 'who is out'. This means the powerful (in this context, 'the government') setting out what they determine something to be at the expense of wider definitions determined by others (in this context, youth workers and young people), who may offer more inclusive and liberating perspectives. Faulks (2000: 2) states that, 'while there is a consensus that citizenship is a desirable thing, there is much less agreement about what the status should entail, what kind of community best promotes citizenship, and whether the status is inherently exclusive'. Given these differences, there is a need for a bounded descriptor that will enable the discussions in this chapter to have context. I propose the following definition, not because it is the most complete and encompassing, but because it provides a coherent framework within which to explore the subject:

> *Citizenship is a relationship of associational identity between an individual and a political community where all citizens have equal rights to participate in that community and equal responsibilities to promote and sustain it.*

A detailed analysis of each policy initiative is not proposed, but the following quotations are offered to illustrate the interplay between citizenship agendas and policy rhetoric:

We are interested in all aspects of a young person's development as active members of their local community, potential parents of the future, fulfilled individuals and members of the workforce.

(DfEE, 2001: 3)

The youth service is well placed to support young people in understanding their rights and responsibilities and to develop as active citizens and participants in our democratic processes.

(DfES, 2002: 3)

The conditions for respect in society are not difficult to define. They depend ultimately on a shared commitment to a common set of values, expressed through behaviour that is considerate of others. Almost everyone of any age and from any community understands what it is and thinks it is right. The values include respect for others, their property and their privacy, civility, good manners and a recognition that everyone has responsibilities as well as rights.

(Respect Task Force, 2006: 5)

Young people will form their own ambitious and pragmatic goals to . . . 'be active in society, taking the initiative and demonstrating leadership to make a positive contribution to local communities and the wider world'.

(DfE, 2011a: 12)

The term 'civil society' is also disputed. It is beyond the scope of this chapter to debate the various definitions, other than to note that:

. . . there has been tension between radical and neo-liberal interpretations of civil society – the former seeing it as a ground from which to challenge the status quo and build alternatives, and the latter as a service-providing, not-for-profit sector necessitated by 'market failure'.

(Edwards, 2009: viii)*

These tensions are highlighted by current economic challenges.

For the purposes of this critique, the work of Edwards provides an apt backdrop and definition of civil society and comprises three elements:

---

* The word, 'radical' in this context meaning resistance to the prevailing systems and more energised and confrontational community activism (Alinsky, 1971).

1. Civil Society as Associational Life – aiming for social, economic and political progress.
2. Civil Society as the Good Society – providing opportunities for people to act together, developing values and skills.
3. Civil Society as the Public Sphere – a space for argument and deliberation that negotiates a sense of the common good.

As such, this definition might be considered a linking narrative between the dynamics of citizenship, civil society and faith-based youth work. Both citizenship and civil society agendas and the aspirations of faith-based youth work find resonance in developing associational life, the good society and a public sphere which represents the common good.

Individual policy initiatives come and go but 'the Big Society' has been seen as offering a conceptual framework for how wider social challenges may be addressed. This example, coupled with the findings of recent research undertaken with faith-based youth workers, is used in this chapter to illustrate the inter-relationship between a fast-changing policy environment and a creative, resilient and enterprising faith-based sector. It explores whether it offers a credible platform upon which citizenship can be enhanced and the common good of civil society developed.

Big Society and Civil Society

The concept of a 'Big Society' found contemporary political expression in the UK from c.2008. Opinions about its value vary widely with some considering it a potential solution to everything that is wrong with Britain (Blond, 2010; Norman, 2010) whilst others view it as a cynical cover for cuts in services, including the decimation of youth work services. For some it is empowering, liberating and brings together ideals of rights, responsibilities and reciprocity that will combine to build stronger and more sustainable communities. Others perceive the concept as controlling, curtailing and lacking in credibility and coherence, believing that it will lead to divisive and unsustainable work with young people, that will only further marginalise those considered 'at risk' (*Common Wealth*, 2010). What is apparent is that 'there is little clear understanding of the Big Society among the public' (House of Commons Public Administration Select Committee, 2011: 1) with little consideration afforded about what it means in respect of young people.

> *The connections between the Big Society agenda and children have not been fully considered. How do we ensure that children and young*

people – often members of a community with only a small voice – can contribute to building and can benefit from safe and friendly communities?

(Fisher and Gruescu, 2011: 4)

The aforementioned Select Committee concluded that Government must increase public understanding of the idea and set out more clearly what it means in practical terms (House of Commons Public Administration Select Committee, 2011: 14).

My own research project, titled The Big View, has indicated that whilst faith-based youth workers are overwhelmingly interested in the Big Society notion (79% expressing moderate to high levels of interest) over 63% said they did not have a good understanding about what it was all about (Pimlott 2011).* For example, Esther (one of the faith-based youth workers in my research) stated 'I don't know what the Big Society is – ain't got a clue' (ibid: 33). Irrespective of the lack of clarity, cynicism about Government motivation is apparent. Graham, another faith-based youth worker, stated 'I am still working on the theory that they haven't worked out the Big Society yet, but they have already done the cuts' (ibid: 35). Notwithstanding such views, the research concluded that there was both optimism and pessimism about the direction of future social policy and that 'the Big Society is already being done by faith-based youth work' (Vijay, faith-based youth worker, ibid: 33).

It is in this fluid and contested context that faith-based youth work currently operates. If the Big Society is to become the process, mechanism and catalyst for civil renewal and ensure that young people develop as citizens who have a considered and meaningful place in society, then the research indicates that more needs to be done by policy-makers to bring clarity and overcome suspicions of ulterior motives; interestingly, the same type of criticism often directed at faith-based work by some secularist and humanistic cohorts (Khan, 2005: 2; Green, 2006: 4).

When it comes to building civil society, the Big Society notion runs the risk of developing as a barrier which prevents it, rather than a mechanism which enables it. If it is perceived as problematic and people don't grasp the concept, or are suspicious of it, the chances of it being an influential agent of

---

* A copy of the full research findings, *The Big View*, can be downloaded from the Frontier Youth Trust web site: www.fyt.org.uk My initial research was undertaken with a wide variety of faith-based youth workers coming from many youth work backgrounds representing a broad cross-section of faith traditions. My latter research focussed upon a series of Christian-motivated projects working inclusively with young people of all faiths and of none.

change look fragile. This was recognised by the faith-based youth workers in my research. For example, John explained 'It could be divisive, lead to greater inequalities in society. It could underline difference – rather than the starting point being what we agree on, it could be what we disagree on' (Pimlott, 2011: 41).

Legitimacy, power and urgency

The Coalition Government's social policy endeavours to build civil society by:

1. Promoting social action.
2. Empowering local communities.
3. Opening up public service contracts.

(Office for Civil Society, 2010: 6)

These three overarching drivers are the closest and clearest indications of what the Big Society means in reality. My research and work with Frontier Youth Trust gives me the privilege of meeting, working with and training many faith-based youth workers. As part of this work, numerous discussions about these objectives have taken place in lecture, seminar and workshop settings with youth workers.

There is compelling anecdotal evidence that faith-based workers have a strong desire for long-term action and social change. They also want to see the empowerment and involvement of local people as part of this process. This is perhaps not surprising given their dual motivations of transformational faith values and empowerment-oriented youth work pedagogies. Indeed, such motivations have been in evidence over many years and faith-based work has pointed toward Big Society type work long before the concept was coined. Cameron himself has asserted that Christians 'would be absolutely right to claim Jesus founded the Big Society 2000 years ago' (Moss, 2011: web). Irrespective of whether or not faith groups want to be associated with this particular expression, other faith groups may well make similar assertions regarding their own founding figures and responses to social needs. The current Chief Rabbi has gone further and contended that 'if you are searching for the Big Society, here's [places of worship] where you may find it' (Sacks, 2011: web). As far back as their re-entry to England in Cromwellian times, Jewish groups in the UK sought to build community and an early version of the 'Big Society' by setting up 'schoolhouses, orphanages, charities for the elderly, blind and disabled, and support for the poor' (Jewish Leadership Council, 2010: 9). The Jewish Leadership Council's CEO, Newman, confidently asserted that the 'entire lexicon of the Big Society could have been drawn from the institutional base of the UK Jewish community' (ibid: 4).

Other immigrant communities have also modelled Big Society notions before the term ever emerged. During my research I visited a Sikh project in Birmingham that operates many community projects and facilities, feeds thousands of people each week, is served by an army of volunteers who give both time and money to operate schools, offers job creation schemes and facilitates work with children, young people and families. It might also be argued that the Church of England report *Faith in The City* (Archbishop of Canterbury's Commission on Urban Priority Areas, 1985) sought to address the very same challenges that the 'Big Society' currently does. In many ways the context for this report was similar to that of today. As the report noted, structural inequalities in society, economic crisis, large-scale unemployment, inner-city housing crisis, and social disintegration were prevalent. In language not dissimilar to that now used about the 'Big Society', the report called for greater consultation with, and participation by, local people at neighbourhood level and a new deal between government and the voluntary sector to ensure long-term work was sustainable. Furthermore, well-established Catholic Social Teaching ideals of solidarity, subsidiarity, human dignity and the common good all underpin the 'Big Society' framework and in many ways point toward it as a response to help build civil society (Ivereigh, 2010; Brandon, 2011: 12–24).

Despite these historical resonances, what is equally clear from my observations is that there is no real appetite for the type of public sector reform currently being introduced by Government in parallel with 'Big Society' rhetoric. There is also very little demand from faith-based youth workers to be 'paid by results' for work that contributes to government objectives and little enthusiasm for commissioned and contracted work.

In my work I have been asking faith-based workers to undertake a simple 'dot-ranking' exercise to express their priorities and preferences against a dozen or so of the key 'Big Society' values. Whilst not a controlled research investigation, this dot ranking exercise has been overwhelming in its conclusions. I estimate that over a thousand 'dot' votes have been cast as part of this process with 'public sector reform' receiving no more than ten of these votes and 'being paid by results' not many more. In contrast, hundreds have been cast for social action and empowerment values. Given these findings, it must be asked if faith-based youth workers will be involved as stakeholders in the more macro elements of the 'Big Society'. Whilst some larger national and regional faith-based youth work organisations might engage, questions remain about the role of local mosques, churches, temples and synagogues in the new cultural paradigms.

In 1997, Mitchell et al. asked some important questions about stakeholders. They analysed 'who' and 'what' really matters in any given situation and devised three key questions concerning legitimacy, power and urgency. It would seem apt to pose these questions here, so that faith-based youth workers can begin to consider the relevance and influence of the 'Big Society' on their work:

1. Legitimacy – is the notion of a 'Big Society' a valid way of responding to the current challenges faced by faith-based youth workers? If so, which elements of the 'Big Society' have particular legitimacy for building civil society?
2. Power – if it is legitimate, to what extent will it produce the desired 'good society' as an associated whole and what role does faith-based youth work have in this?
3. Urgency – if it is legitimate and likely to be effective, how immediate is the need to be directly (or more) involved with the 'Big Society'?

Even if precise answers to these questions could be achieved, it is unclear what the 'Big Society' idea will do to address the issues of poverty and inequality that so scar our nation and which impact particularly on the current generation of young unemployed people. Whilst Blond (2010: 205–208) is very clear that there needs to be a new economic order to 'recapitalise the poor', current policy initiatives fail to address these key points. Instead, policy tends to focus on measures for getting people into work that, at best, bring about only short-term improvements, not the long-term systemic change that Blond argues will deliver the virtuous, moral, common good 'society we desire' (ibid: 208). There is a fear, summed up by previous Archbishop of Canterbury Rowan Williams, that the 'Big Society' rhetoric is simply 'aspirational waffle designed to conceal a deeply damaging withdrawal of the state from its responsibilities to the most vulnerable' (Williams, 2012: 266).

At the heart of faith-based approaches to civil society and developing the common good is a demand for solidarity with the poor and vulnerable and a response to their needs. Each faith teaches that this is vitally important and many faith-based youth work projects actively work with those young people most at risk by responding to their specific needs. Whilst it may be too early to form fully informed conclusions, there is emerging evidence that it is those who are affluent, white, educated and over sixty-five years old who are most engaged with 'Big Society' aspirations, while those living in deprived and rural areas, from ethnic minorities and under thirty-five are the least engaged (Slocock, 2012: 57–64). If this remains true, there is a risk for those young people in greatest need that poverty and inequality will increase rather than being alleviated. It remains unclear as to whether or not faith-based youth work providers can, should, or will, rise up to fill the gaps left by the withdrawal of the state.

National Citizen Service

Within the overall framework of the Big Society, the advent of National Citizen Service (NCS) is the most recent example of a coherent approach to promoting citizenship and developing civil society with and for young people. It was described as something that will:

> . . . act as a gateway to the Big Society for many young people by supporting them to develop the skills and attitudes they need to become more engaged with their communities and become active and responsible citizens. NCS will make a positive contribution to local communities, requiring close working with schools, local authorities, businesses and other neighbourhood groups to create a more cohesive, responsible and engaged society.
>
> NCS is a voluntary eight-week summer programme for 16-year-olds that will promote:
> - a more cohesive society by mixing participants of different backgrounds
> - a more responsible society by supporting the transition into adulthood for young people
> - a more engaged society by enabling young people to work together to create social action projects in their local communities.
>
> (DfE, 2011b: web)

The NCS embodies many of the new mantras associated with Big Society rhetoric: citizenship, volunteering, young people's participation, social action, community engagement and development, and cohesive association all feature highly. When compared to the definition of civil society put forward by Edwards, and outlined earlier in this chapter, there is a degree of symmetry. Where the comparison perhaps breaks down is in the extent young people will be allowed to engage in 'broad-based debate (that) can define the public interest, not diktats by government. Such debates are the very stuff of democracy' (Edwards, 2009: 65).

While NCS in its present format might sow some new or additional seeds regarding citizenship, it would appear somewhat naive that the stated objectives of cohesion, responsibility and engagement can be achieved in just eight weeks. As the head of policy at YMCA England, Jason Stacey, rightly asserts: 'there are 52 weeks in a year. Where do they (young people) go on a cold November night when they want something to do?' (cited by Williams, 2011: web).

In a manner perhaps typical of the Coalition Government's approach to many policy initiatives, the scheme has been introduced at break-neck speed whilst other valuable and commended existing work has been cut, closed, or simply re-branded. In the process of trying to develop citizenship and build civil society it has dismantled many long-term pieces of work that had proven track records of achieving these objectives, and instead has implemented a short-term scheme that has no evidence to support the claims it makes. It sought to strengthen the voluntary sector, bypassing local authorities.

Its approach to construction and funding caused the House of Commons Education Select Committee to conclude that it could not 'support the continued development of the NCS in its current form' (House of Commons Education Select Committee, 2011: 60). Deeming it a worthy aspiration but very expensive, it advised that funds earmarked for NCS should be 'diverted into year-round youth services' (ibid: 61).

The NCS may have been a good additional service for young people, but not the 'instead of' programme that it appears to have become. What role faith and spirituality have in the NCS programme remains unclear. Some faith-based providers have successfully tendered for NCS delivery contracts, but the organisations awarded delivery contracts reveals a list dominated by large regional and national bodies rather than local faith organisations. This is perhaps inevitable given the approach and mechanisms employed, but somewhat paradoxical given the stated agendas in favour of localism and empowerment.

Commodification

The Big View research and subsequent conversations with workers have also been highly critical of policy agendas that continually commodify work with young people. Whilst commissioning, tendering, procurement, payment by results and talk of social investment bonds proliferate at policy level, they seem to have little support in many faith-based settings.

This trend toward putting a price on everything has gathered momentum in the last few decades. As Chris Ruane, MP (2012) noted:

> . . . *something happened in the 1980s. The Government often talk about the broken society and broken Britain, but I honestly believe that the problem started to ramp up in the "loadsamoney" era, when there was no such thing as society and atomisation and isolation were rampant. We have also seen the decline of those institutions that did believe in a big society and in social cohesion, such as the Church and the trade unions. Stable minds equal a stable society, but even Labour used the terms "producer" and "consumer". We did not use "citizen", and that is what we need to get back to – to viewing individuals as citizens and as part of society.*
>
> (Ruane, 2012: Hansard)

The proclaimed benefits of efficiency, value for money and the opportunity to get new, paid work previously undertaken by Government do not sit easily within themes of the Big Society. While the rhetoric endeavours to build community between people, develop mutuality, reciprocity, the common good, and citizenship, the reality is often competition between providers, a 'race to the bottom' (Nicholls, 2012) short-term approaches, disjointed post-code lottery provision and a lack of trust within and across youth work service providers. The market capitalism mechanisms on offer risk undermining the very aspirations they were intended to fulfil.

For Glasman (2011) this heightened commodification is one of the perils of the Coalition policy framework. Things and people that 'were originally not for sale, are now for sale'. Contracts are awarded and work commissioned predominantly via economic mechanisms, not relationships and reciprocity. Decisions that used to be based upon need are now based upon money. Capitalism has put a value on many of the processes and mechanisms that define civil society and turned them into commodities. These approaches have been heavily criticised in welfare and health policy contexts, but have proceeded almost un-critiqued in youth work arenas.

Whilst current Government guidance on 'Best Value' talks of 'economic, environmental and social value', it is within the potentially paradoxical duty to operate with 'economy, efficiency and effectiveness' (Department for

Communities and Local Government, 2011: 6). It is the lack of stated clarity over defining these terms that often seems to give precedent to economic judgements alone,* ignoring wider spiritual, ethical, long-term and holistic well-being considerations, which are often the more significant drivers of faith-based youth work practice.

Reflecting on how these commodifying approaches have come to dominate in the United States, Giroux (2011) comments:

> *At the heart of this market rationality is an egocentric philosophy and a culture of cruelty that sells off public goods and services to the highest bidders in the private sector, while simultaneously dismantling those public spheres, social protections and institutions serving the public good. As economic power succeeds in detaching itself from government regulations, a new global financial class reasserts the prerogatives of capital and systemically destroys those public spheres that traditionally advocated for social equality and an educated citizenry as the fundamental conditions for a viable democracy.*

> (Giroux, 2011: web)

The indications are that the UK is on a similar destructive trajectory. There have been calls for a return to a more philanthropic age (Bishop and Green, 2009) but these have also often been clothed in commodification rhetoric rather than compassionate concern. Philanthropy risks becoming synonymous with 'the privatisation and disestablishment of state-run public services . . . a refashioning of the voluntary sector . . . according to the financial tools, language and mentality of modern capitalism' (Kennedy, 2011: web) rather than the virtuous, often faith inspired, dynamic it once was.

Clearly, some faith-based groups have never sought nor taken government funding so they, income allowing, will no doubt simply carry on with their work with young people as they did before these new policy developments. However, if others are to engage in the new economics of this austere age, certain risks need to be considered, assessed and evaluated.

Avoiding mission creep

The medieval legend of the Pied Piper captures it succinctly – 'he who pays the piper calls the tune'. Being funded by an external body carries some risks

---

* For example, many Local Authority youth centres have been closed on economic grounds with little consideration given to long-term social, community development, participation and environmental considerations.

for the faith or voluntary organisation. The funder might be calling a different tune to the one envisaged or they may change the tune mid performance.

Many years ago, Charles Handy addressed this scenario when he stated that many organisations:

> . . . have found themselves agents of their paymasters, be those pay-masters a government department (or a) local authority. Having no clear goals or precise definitions of the task to be done leaves the door open to what amounts to a take over. What price democracy and voluntarism when he who pays the piper is free to call the tune?
>
> (Handy, 1988: 7)

Luke Bretherton also highlights the challenges associated with being funded by external stakeholders, the most notable being the threat of 'institutional isomorphism'. This is 'a process where religious organisations reshape themselves to fit government policy and thereby lose their unique characteristics, while taking on the same institutional shape and processes as state agencies' (2010: 41–2). In youth work terms this concept is evidenced by 'funding streams tied to policies concerned with the control and safeguarding of young people rather than their development' (Davies and Merton, 2009: 46). In short, faith-based youth workers obtaining such funding potentially have to prefer working to government policies, as a priority over and above objectives set by their own mission.[*]

In detailing three domains, DiMaggio and Powell (1983) describe how institutional isomorphism materialises:

1. **Coercion** – where work is compelled to become what, in this context, government thinks it should be. Examples of this here would be the presumptions seemingly made by the Coalition Government that every voluntary organisation: wants to grow, wants to bid for contracts from central Government, thinks getting paid by results is a good idea, is driven by economic imperatives and wishes to align itself with Big Society ideologies.
2. **Mimicking** – where faith organisations feel compelled to copy what others are doing. Examples here might include: developing partnership work because everybody else is doing so, spending significant resources on marketing, web sites and the like with little evidence that this expenditure brings any benefits to a local group, adopting an outcomes approach

---

[*] Some elements of some faith groups choose not to seek government funding.

to work that risks, 'dehumanizing the whole of youth work engagement' (Belton, 2012: 226) and positively responding to invitations to continually 'do more for less' (Cameron, 2010).

3. **Normative pressures** – where pressure from professionals embed a set of expectations that shape work. Examples might include: the professionalisation of youth work, the growth of accredited training and qualifications, the rise of expert consultants to tell local people how to do faith-based youth work and pressure to do 'youth work' rather than 'youth ministry'.*

The examples quoted are not necessarily bad in themselves and engagement with these considerations may be appropriate for some faith-based work. One of the projects involved in my research runs a Level 2 youth work course for its community volunteers and senior young people. Operating the course to state-orchestrated standards and frameworks and receiving state funding to do so would not per se represent an isomorphic threat as it would not compromise the objectives of the organisation. Similarly, running a summer programme of activities in the local park for local young people funded by the state would not necessarily represent a threat as long as the programme was shaped by the young people and the organisation delivering it and was not simply a charade aimed at meeting the latest Local Authority targets and outcomes.

Sometimes funding comes with strings attached and faith-based organisations need to make value judgements against their own charitable objectives and missional aims before deciding whether or not to accept such funding. A few years ago a drop-in project I was involved in received a small grant for some tables and chairs. The drop-in was staffed mainly by Christian volunteers, but virtually all the young people who attended had no particular faith allegiance. The funder stipulated that the chairs and tables could not be used to support any faith work. I was never sure what to do if an ad hoc conversation with young person over a cup of coffee about faith or spirituality took place. Did I need to ask them to stand up and take their mug of coffee off the table?

Over time this particular project won over the hearts and minds of local policy-makers and they began to see the faith dynamic as a positive attribute rather than a risk. The project even began to influence local approaches to policy and, as further funding came to the project, broad-based partnership work developed and a sense of reciprocal mutuality ensued. This was built

---

* See the chapter also in this book by Jon Jolly.

upon trusting relationships with everybody working together to achieve the best for local young people. My research has confirmed these dynamics as key components of faith-based work.

A number of key questions need to be asked by practitioners before offers are considered, before engagement is undertaken, and before invitations accepted. These include:

- Is the faith-based youth work I am involved in called to work in these ways?
- Do the values of the other bodies I am proposing working with resonate with my own values?
- Will engagement with the agendas of others help fulfil the mission of my work?
- Will employing the methods of others help achieve my aims?
- Does the ethical base of my faith-based youth work allow me to engage in these ways of working?
- Do the young people I work with want to work in these ways and according to these agendas?
- Should my faith-based youth work be shaped or influenced by Government agendas at all or should I be setting my own counter-cultural course according to my own faith beliefs?

If these questions are not addressed then, as Bretherton comments, faith groups will end up in a position where ministry is distorted and witness is re-moulded around the instrumental requirements of the state (2010: 45). Anecdotal evidence indicates this 'mission creep'* (Davies, 2012: 168) appears well-established in faith-based youth work, which if not addressed and responded to, will allow distortions to erode the distinctiveness of the work, potentially rendering it no different from any other type of youth work.[†]

Conclusion

The Big Society is the latest attempt to develop civil society and restore a sense of civic purpose in the UK. It has been portrayed as a quick fix response to current societal challenges, but Government ministers have been clear that it is a 'generational' long-term 20 year plus project designed to bring about embedded cultural change (House of Commons Public Administration Committee,

---

* Originally a military term, but now applied more widely with particular reference to not for profit organisations.

† This tendency is highlighted by Cressey (2007).

2011: 74, 93). If this is the case and it is successful in achieving such a change then it will impact all work with young people.

Building civil society continues to be a cultural imperative in a society where young people are deemed to have no stake in the nation (Singh et al., 2011: 13). Developing citizenship amongst young people needs to be a considered and vital element of this task. It seems hugely optimistic to expect that this can be achieved via something like a short-term summer programme especially when this seems to be prescribed 'top-down' rather than democratically negotiated with young people. When this rationale is considered alongside huge cuts in local, year-round services the outlook does not appear particularly positive. Faith-based youth work might be one of the few elements of youth work which remains tangibly active and visible in local communities.

In order to retain its integrity and focus, faith-based workers need to work from their own unique values and sense of mission. This is confirmed by my research (Pimlott, 2011) and implies an imperative that such work needs to remain distinctive as part of its contribution to the common good. Becoming like everybody else will serve no purpose. This doesn't require an isolationist approach, but rather one that works with policy makers and other practitioners alike, on terms mutually considered and not imposed. Whether others will be inspired to listen to such a perspective remains open to question.

In the meantime, faith-based workers will no doubt continue to build civil society irrespective, and sometimes in spite of, policy makers. After all, faith groups have been building the Big Society for hundreds and, in some cases, thousands of years.

References

Alinsky, S.D. (1971) *Rules for Radicals*. New York: Vintage.

Archbishop of Canterbury's Commission on Urban Priority Areas (1985) *Faith in The City*. London: Church House Publishing.

Banks, S. (2010) *Ethical Issues in Youth Work*. Abingdon: Routledge.

Belton, B. (2012) Youth Work and Islam: A Growing Tradition? In Ahmad, F. and Seddon, M.S. (Eds.) *Muslim Youth: Challenges, Opportunities and Expectations*. London: Continuum International Publishing Group.

Bishop, M. and Green, M. (2009) *Philanthrocapitalism: How Giving Can Save The World*. New York: Bloomsbury Press.

Blond, P. (2010) *Red Tory. How Left and Right Have Broken Britain and How We Can Fix it*. London: Faber and Faber.

Brandon, G. (2011) *The Big Society in Context: A Means to What End?* Cambridge: The Jubilee Centre.

Bretherton, L. (2010) *Christianity and Contemporary Politic*. Chichester: Wiley-Blackwell.

Cameron, D. (2009) *The Big Society.* Hugo Young Lecture, London, 10 November 2009.

Cameron, D. (2010) *Good Government Costs Less With the Conservatives.* Speech to Conservative Party Welsh Conference, Llandudno, 6 March 2010.

Common Wealth (2010) *The Big Society or The Big Lie?* London: Common Wealth. http://www. ekklesia.co.uk/CommonWealthStatement.

Cressey, G. (2007) Youth Work, With Muslim Young Women: The Ultimate Separatist Cage? *Youth and Policy,* 92, 33–46.

Davies, B. and Merton, B. (2009) *Squaring the Circle? Findings of a "Modest Inquiry" Into The State of Youth Work Practice in a Changing Policy Environment.* Leicester: De Montfort University. http://www.dmu.ac.uk/documents/health-and-life-sciences-documents/research/squaringth-ecircle.pdf.

Davies, S. (2012) The Management of Faith Based Youth Work. In Ord, J. (Ed.) *Critical Issues in Youth Work Management.* Abingdon: Routledge.

Department for Communities and Local Government (2011) *Best Value Statutory Guidance.* London: DfCLG.

Department for Education (2011a) *Positive for Youth: A New Approach to Cross-Government Policy For Young People Aged 13 to 19.* London: Department for Education. http://media.edu-cation.gov.uk/assets/files/pdf/p/positive%20for%20youth.pdf.

Department for Education (2011b) *National Citizen Service.* London: Department for Education. http://www.education.gov.uk/childrenandyoungpeople/youngpeople/nationalcitizenservice/a0075357/national-citizen-service.

Department for Education and Employment (2001) *Transforming Youth Work. Developing Youth Work For Young People.* London: Department for Education and Employment/Connexions.

Department for Education and Skills (2002) *Transforming Youth Work – Resourcing Excellent Youth Services.* London: Department for Education and Skills/Connexions.

Di Maggio, P.J. and Powell, W. (1983) The Iron Cage Revisited: Institutional Isomorphism and Collective Rationality in Organizational Fields. *American Sociological Review,* 48, 147–60. http://www.ics.uci.edu/~corps/phaseii/DiMaggioPowell-IronCageRevisited-ASR.pdf.

Edwards, M. (2009) *Civil Society.* Cambridge: Polity Press.

Faulks, K. (2000) *Citizenship.* London: Routledge.

Fisher, D. and Gruesco, S. (2011) *Big Society and Children: Backing Communities to Keep The Next Generation Safe and Happy.* London: ResPublica and Action for Change. http://respublica.org.uk/documents/dlo_ResPublica%20Children%20and%20the%20Big%20Society.pdf.

Fitzsimons, A., Hope, M., Cooper, C. and Russell, K. (2011) *Empowerment and Participation in Youth Work.* Exeter: Learning Matters.

Giroux, H.A. (2011) *Youth in a Suspect Society: Coming of Age in an Era of Disposability.* Truth-Out.Org, 5 May 2011. http://www.truth-out.org/youth-suspect-society-coming-age-era-disposability/1304604010.

Glasman, M. (2011) *Civil Society.* Speech at 'Big Society – Bigger Nature', Manchester, 1 October 2011, Lincoln Theological Institute/University of Manchester.

Green, M. (2006) *A Journey of Discovery – Spirituality and Spiritual Development in Youth Work.* Leicester: National Youth Agency.

Green, M. (2010) Youth Worker as Converters: Ethical Issues in Faith-Based Youth Work. In Banks, S. (Ed.) *Ethical Issues in Youth Work.* Abingdon: Routledge.

Handy, C. (1988) *Understanding Voluntary Organisations.* London: Penguin Books.

House of Commons Education Select Committee (2011) *Services for Young People: Third Report of Session 2010–2011, Volume 1.* London: HMSO.

House of Commons Public Administration Select Committee (2011) *The Big Society: Seventeenth Report of Session 2010–2012, Volume 1.* London: HMSO.

Ivereigh, A. (2010) *Faithful Citizens: A Practical Guide to Catholic Social Teaching and Community Organising.* London: Darton, Longman and Todd.

Jewish Leadership Council (2010) *The Big Society and the UK Jewish Community.* London: The Jewish Leadership Council.

Kennedy, J. (2011) *New Bosses, New Control Agenda.* London: Directory of Social Change. http://www.dsc.org.uk/PolicyandResearch/News/Newbossesnewcontrolagenda.

Khan, M.G. (2005) Towards a National Strategy for Muslim Youth Work. *Youth and Policy,* 92, 7–18.

Mitchell, R.K., Agle, B.R. and Wood, D.J. (1997) Toward a Theory of Stakeholder Identification and Salience: Defining The Principle of Who and What Really Counts. *Academy of Management Review,* 22: 4, 853–86.

Moss, V. (2011) Fury as David Cameron Claims Jesus Founded his Big Society Crusade. *Sunday Mirror,* 22 May 2011. http://www.mirror.co.uk/news/top-stories/2011/05/22/fury-as-david-cameron-claims-jesus-founded-his-big-society-crusade-115875-23146993/.

Nicholls, D. (2012) *For Youth Workers and Youth Work.* Bristol: Policy Press.

Norman, J. (2010) *The Big Society: The Anatomy of The New Politics.* Buckingham: The University of Buckingham Press.

Office for Civil Society (2010) *Supporting A Stronger Civil Society.* London: Office for Civil Society.

Pimlott, N. (2011) *The Big View: Faith-Based Youth Work and the Big Society.* Birmingham: Frontier Youth Trust. www.fyt.org.uk.

Respect Task Force (2006) *Respect Action Plan.* London: Home Office and Respect Task Force.

Ruane, C. (2012) House of Commons: Hansard Debates 24 January 2012. *Children's Subjective Well-Being.* http://www.publications.parliament.uk/pa/cm201212/cmhansrd/cm120124/debtext/120124-0004.htm#1201251000070.

Sacks, J. (2011) If You Are Searching For The Big Society, Here's Where You May Find it. *New Statesman,* 13 June 2011. http://www.newstatesman.com/religion/2011/06/religious-community-social.

Singh, D. et al. (Eds.) (2011) *Five Days in August: Interim Report of the 2011 English Riots.* London: Riots Panel. http://www.5daysinaugust.co.uk/PDF/downloads/Interim-Report-UK-Riots.pdf.

Slocock, C. (2012) The *Big Society Audit 2012.* London: Civil Exchange, Democratic Audit and DHA Communications.

Williams, R. (2011) Will the National Citizen Service Stop Young People Rioting? *The Guardian,* 30 August 2011. http://www.guardian.co.uk/society/2011/aug/30/national-citizen-service-prevent-rioting.

Williams, R. (Rowan) (2012) *Faith in the Public Square.* London: Bloomsbury Continuum.

CHAPTER 6

Sex Talk: Discussion and Meaning-making Among Religious Young Adults

Sarah-Jane Page

Where does discussion about sex and sexuality take place for religious young adults? How well do religious young people feel they know the perspectives and debates within their religious tradition regarding sexuality? This chapter, based on a project which studied 18–25 year olds from a variety of religious traditions, will examine the context in which sexuality was discussed, giving particular attention to religious spaces, significant individuals (e.g. parents and friends) and popular media. The concluding section will also highlight some points for youth work practice, based on the perspectives of young people.

Previous research has indicated that young people are not given the right resources for learning about sexuality in parental and formal educational contexts (Allen, 2005; Averett et al., 2009). Allen has discussed the gaps in secular school-based sex education, which tends to offer only a perfunctory overview of disease- and pregnancy-avoidance. Biological issues are privileged over feelings and desires, lest such a focus would encourage young people to become sexually active. Meanwhile, Averett et al. have focused on the role of parents in sex education, finding that parents are often unwilling to discuss sex with their children. Rather, media outlets – such as reality TV, films and teen magazines – as well as peer groups – become the principal sources of information about sexuality for young people (Durham, 2002; Epstein et al., 2003; Johansson, 2007; Kehily, 2002).

As a location for the dissemination and articulation of moral values, religious institutions can be considered prime spaces in which learning about sexuality takes place, but research indicates that here, too, young people receive fragmentary messages, with media outlets often becoming an alternative source of knowledge for religious youth (Cooksey and Dooms, 2010; Regnerus, 2007).

The study on which this chapter is based considered six religions – Buddhism, Christianity, Hinduism, Islam, Judaism and Sikhism – as well as mixed-faith individuals (e.g. 'Muslim-Christian').* All the young people who participated were aged between 18 and 25 and lived in the UK. The research was conducted using three sequential methods. Firstly, an online questionnaire where participants were sought through a number of different outlets such as places of worship, religious youth groups, secular youth societies, lesbian, gay, bisexual and trans (LGBT) groups, university societies, magazines, on-line forums, and advertisements generated through Facebook. In total, 693 young people completed the questionnaire.† The second and third stages of the research involved interviews and video diaries, and were comprised of diverse samples of 61 and 24 individuals respectively.

At the questionnaire stage, participants were asked to rank five factors that influenced their sexual values and attitudes, as well as their sexual practices. A number of factors could be selected, which coalesced around three broad themes – religion (religious texts; religious faith; religious leaders), relational influences (parents; siblings; other relatives; friends) and media (the internet, electronic media such as TV, printed media such as magazines). The list was not intended to be exhaustive, and participants were able to outline additional factors. The respondents' first choices regarding what mainly influenced their sexual values and attitudes as well as their sexual practices are featured in Table 6.1. Table 6.2 reports the influences when all five factors are taken into account.

In the interviews and video diaries, further information was elicited on these themes. Each theme will now be taken in turn and discussed in more depth, with a focus on religious influences, relational influences, and mediated influences.

* The project entitled *Religion, Youth and Sexuality: A Multi-faith Exploration*, was funded by the Arts and Humanities Research Council/Economic and Social Research Council *Religion and Society* Programme (Award no. AH/G014051/1). The research team consisted of Prof. Andrew Kam-Tuck Yip (Principal Investigator), Dr. Michael Keenan (Co-investigator) and Dr. Sarah-Jane Page (Research Fellow). The research team is grateful for the funding, as well as the invaluable contribution of the respondents, individuals and groups who helped with the recruitment of the sample and the members of the advisory committee.

† The sample composition: 57.1% Christian, 16.6% Muslim, 7.5% Jewish, 6.8% Hindu, 4.5% Buddhist, 3.8% Sikh, 3.7% mixed faith, e.g. Christian-Muslim. 65.7% were women. 74.3% identified as heterosexual, 10% as lesbian, gay or homosexual, 7.5% as bisexual and 5.9% who specifically decided to not define their sexual orientation. Other participants indicated their own preferred category, such as queer, bicurious and asexual.

Table 6.1 Participants' top factors in what they felt most influences their sexual values and attitudes[1]/sexual practices[2]

Source of influence	Sexual values and attitudes (%)	Sexual practices (%)
Religious faith	46.0	43.1
Parents	15.8	9.4
Friends	14.0	16.0
Religious texts	11.5	10.4
Media[3]	4.3	10.2
Religious leaders	1.1	1.0
Other factors[4]	7.3	9.9
TOTAL	100	100

[1] The total number of valid cases is 530.

[2] The total number of valid cases is 489.

[3] Comprising the choices, 'the internet', 'electronic media' and 'printed media'. These three choices have been presented together, in order to demonstrate the strength of the 'media' category as a whole, for to separate the factors dilutes 'media', underplaying its significance.

[4] Other factors included siblings, other relatives, partner, intellectual knowledge, among others, but individually they comprised a very small share of the overall influences.

Table 6.2 What participants felt influences sexual values and attitudes[1]/sexual practices[2] drawing on all five factors

Source of influence	Sexual values and attitudes (%)	Sexual practices (%)
Religious faith	18.2	17.6
Parents	15.3	12.6
Friends	16.5	16.1
Religious texts	12.8	12.7
Media[3]	16.8	21.1
Religious leaders	8.5	8.5
Other factors[4]	11.9	11.4
TOTAL	100	100

[1] The total number of valid cases is 2316 (participants could select up to five choices, so are multiply counted).

[2] The total number of valid cases is 2069 (participants could select up to five choices, so are multiply counted).

[3] Comprising the choices, 'the internet', 'electronic media' and 'printed media'. These three choices have been presented together, in order to demonstrate the strength of the 'media' category as a whole, for to separate the factors dilutes 'media', underplaying its significance.

[4] Other factors included siblings, other relatives, partner, intellectual knowledge, among others, but individually they comprised a very small share of the overall influences.

Religious resources: texts, faith and leaders

When articulating what they felt influenced their sexual values and attitudes, religious faith was the first choice for 46% of participants. Religious texts and religious leaders had less impact, sharing 11.5% and 1.1% of the first choices respectively. However, on taking all five main factors into account, religious faith made up 18.2% of all factors, compared with 8.5% for religious leaders and 12.8% for religious texts. As Tables 6.1 and 6.2 indicate, the results were similar for the question regarding what influenced their sexual practices.

The extent to which young adults learned about sexuality from religious spaces (institutions and religious leaders) was mixed. A dominant theme was that discussions around sexuality tended to be transitory, occurring infrequently or not at all, as Adam explained:

> *You might have the occasional lesson at Evensong . . . St. Paul's teaching on fornication, but nine times out of ten the preacher will choose the other text to preach about and that lesson will fade back into obscurity for another year.*
>
> (Heterosexual Christian man, interview)

Yasmin emphasised the general reluctance for sexual topics to be discussed at the Islamic Saturday School she attended – all the more pertinent for she was gaining a qualification, part of which covered the Islamic understandings of sexuality:

> *Our exam was in a few days . . . we went up to [the teacher] and asked him, well what's the answer, and he was very short and he basically said that contraception is forbidden in Islam . . . there was no explanation as to why it was forbidden . . . Other questions like the oneness of God we spent weeks upon.*
>
> (Chose not to define her sexuality, Muslim woman, interview)

Sexuality was often given a taboo status and discussion in this area was not supported. Abby's experience, a Jewish lesbian, was more the exception; she said that leaflets about sexuality were prominently displayed in her synagogue. However, she later reflected that sexuality was not embedded in faith discussion, saying 'it's not really been spoken about'.

Despite the fleeting nature of religious instruction, *most* participants came away with a sense of the religious 'rules' relating to sexuality – for example, whether there were prohibitions relating to sex outside of marriage. Ranjit said:

When I went to Sunday school . . . we never spoke about such things. Even now, we still run the Sunday school for these kids and we never talk about such things . . . We're trying to inculcate the values of Hinduism and that means telling them what Hinduism is all about . . . why certain beliefs are carried out . . . I've never actually had any conversation or had anyone tell me this really . . . I think it's just the environment and my surroundings which directed me in that belief.

(Heterosexual Hindu man, interview)

As Elias (1982) has theorised, value transmission is often not fully concretised in the minds of individuals. Gestures play as much of a part as words in the transmission of values from one generation of religious adults to the next. For example, Freitas (2008) has described that in America, giving a silver ring to a teenager (denoting chastity until marriage) becomes a symbol for parental attitude towards sex. The problem Freitas outlines, however, is that such symbols become substitutes for actually talking about sexual matters. This can lead to misinformation and miscommunication. In our study, it was quite common for young adults to be either confused about or simply to not know their faith's position on certain issues, particularly homosexuality. Surjit said:

I could never associate from what the Sikh point of view on sex is such and such, because it was never in my mind put together in those kind of sort of structured format, you know, whether it's from my parents or the Gurdwara, there had never been a discussion on the issue.

(Heterosexual Sikh woman, interview)

Akin to Freitas's (2008) research, such individuals appear to learn about sexuality through a process of osmosis – there is a general understanding of key ideas (e.g. no sex before marriage) but this is not underpinned by discussion about why such positions are taken. Participants could be engaging in practices not condoned by their religious group (Cooksey and Dooms, 2010). Jodie, a bisexual Orthodox Jewish woman, embarked on a two-year relationship with another young woman. Although throughout the relationship she had the feeling 'that something is wrong with this', she had had little discussion about what the Orthodox Jewish position was on this issue. From her knowledge that sex was to be within marriage only, she said that 'it was easier for me to ignore what I was doing with a girl because, well, that's not actually sex, I mean Halachically,* it doesn't count as sex you know, I'm still a

---

* As pertaining to Jewish law

virgin'. But a debate about homosexuality within her community erupted on the blogosphere, and immersing herself in this discussion influenced Jodie's decision to terminate her sexual relationship. The debate had generated a variety of perspectives and opinions – both liberal and conservative – but after taking stock of the situation, Jodie decided that 'It would be too difficult for me to attempt to maintain anything like that [relationship] long term, and it just didn't fit in with my vision of how I was going to fit in with the Jewish community, which was in a traditional manner'.

Faith leaders who did discuss sex and sexuality in authoritative forums (e.g. sermons) could be extremely influential in helping young adults make sense of theory and practice. One of the opening sermons given to students at Mark's university helped him make sense of his beliefs in relation to appropriate practice:

> *[The pastor said that] we as young adults will draw a line, we will say anything up to that line is ok and anything after isn't until marriage. Some people will draw it at foreplay, other people will draw it right up to, but not including, penetration, and then he was like, 'I want to tell you what the Bible said; sexual action is supposed to be saved until marriage and nothing up to that point'. For me hearing that coming from [someone] able to speak on the Bible authoritatively, to then stand up and say this, completely confirmed in me that what I was doing was wrong.*
>
> (Heterosexual Christian man, interview)

This direct teaching gave Mark a distinct set of rules to follow, which he found comforting. At the same time, although the message was clear, if few strategies were given regarding how to live up to these expectations, this could cause further distress and ambiguity for individuals, as Fergus discussed:

> *I don't think [young people] really had the techniques. They were just sort of told if they were in a relationship, you know, to only go as far as holding hands.*
>
> (Heterosexual Christian-Buddhist man, interview)

Direct and uncompromising messages were not favoured by individuals who held alternative theologies. Emily expressed in interview how she had been turned off by this kind of narrative:

> *I was really kind of disillusioned as a teenager with all the more evangelical stuff . . . Kept going to youth events with more evangelical*

tones and just really felt uncomfortable. So suddenly being in this church, it was, 'Ah I can ask all these questions and have all these debates' . . . I think that if the church hadn't been so liberal I would have left.

(Heterosexual Christian woman, interview)

Some young adults felt religious leaders were very engaged with youth issues around sexuality and felt very comfortable discussing their problems. For instance, Tim found talking to his priest a reassuring experience:

He said that he thought that masturbating once or twice a day was quite normal . . . But masturbating more than that, four times or more, was probably unhealthy . . . it was good to hear him just kind of, you know, say very clearly that . . . masturbating excessively is very different from masturbating a few times in a week.

(Heterosexual Buddhist-Christian man, video diary)

On a more negative note, however, other young adults felt a level of embarrassment in approaching faith leaders. For instance, Isma (a heterosexual Muslim woman) said 'You wouldn't actually go to the religious leader per se because some of them are still a bit funny about talking to women and stuff like that'. Crucial in Isma's account was how her faith leader did not create a comfortable atmosphere for her even to pose her queries. The perception was that as a man, he problematised talking to young women about intimate issues.

Consistent with other research (Coleman and Testa, 2008; Freitas, 2008; Sharma, 2011) there was also a feeling by some participants that they would be judged or misunderstood by faith leaders, as Dharam articulated:

I don't see the value in kind of discussing it openly . . . they will just get angry . . . [my viewpoint] is different, but they won't see it like that; a lot of people will just kind of see it as an attack on their belief so there is no value really in kind of trying to explain to them.

(Heterosexual Sikh man, interview)

Dharam felt his religious leaders were too closed-minded to discuss alternative perspectives. This is despite the fact that religious young adults in our sample prized the cultivation of such debates. One issue that participants fielded more discussion on was the ethics around homosexuality, especially in a cultural climate where homosexuality is more likely to be accepted (McAndrew, 2010; Weeks, 2007). This was heightened for LGBT individuals. Stephen, a gay

Christian, for example, emphasised the difficulties of disclosing his sexuality, with a fear of the repercussions, saying '[My priest] struggles very much with what to do with gay people . . . which is why I haven't told any of them'.

Even though a number of concerns were raised about learning and debate around sexuality in the religious context, it was significant that the top factor participants felt were influencing both attitudes and values, as well as practices, was religious faith. What the participants meant by religious faith could be hard to pin down, but it certainly captures a more individualised relationship to sexual knowledge and practice (Yip and Page, 2013). Indeed, in light of the unsatisfactory experiences many participants had encountered in places of worship, participants put emphasis on the strategies and spaces they created for themselves. Clare, a heterosexual Christian woman, discussed resources such as books (e.g. *Sex God* by Rob Bell), as well as independent reading of the Bible. She was careful not to take what religious leaders said at face value, her own practice being to 'take your Bible with you and read what they're quoting so we can know they're not just talking rubbish'.

Some had fashioned their own youth groups in faith spaces in order to create a proactive environment where sexuality could be discussed. For example, faith groups at university were sometimes seen as important spaces for debate and discussion. Isma, a heterosexual Muslim woman, said that at her university's Islamic Society, 'We talk about what the religion says, what is forbidden, what is allowed, what is it all about, what does it involve. So my understandings are formed by that'. Stuart had created an accountability group with his male Christian friends who were struggling with certain sexual issues such as masturbation:

> I said to a couple of guys there, 'I personally would find this useful; I think we should set this up . . . We need to have a guys' accountability group' . . . We meet up about once a week. And we hold each other accountable.
>
> (Bisexual Christian man, interview)

Such examples demonstrate the resourcefulness of our participants, despite an unsatisfactory response from official faith channels. Using their own resources, through creating their own discussion networks or undertaking an individual quest focused on sacred text examination, allowed these young adults to forge a religiously-inspired understanding of sexuality (Bragg and Buckingham, 2009; Regnerus, 2007). However, it was much rarer for LGBT participants to engage with similar support endeavours with their peers. For example, Stuart, as a bisexual, was able to conform to a heterosexist agenda over the issue of masturbation, but he felt less comfortable disclosing his sexual orientation to fellow Christians, showing the multiple ways in which support was negotiated. Although masturbation was a topic that was on the agenda within his 'accountability group', other issues, namely non-heterosexuality, were not.

Relational resources: parents and friends

Parents were high on the list of participants' perceptions of who influenced their sexual values and attitudes, comprising 15.3% of all factors (they were the first choice for 15.8% of participants). Meanwhile, friends comprised 16.5% of all the factors, but were less likely to be first choice (14.0%). Friends were also more likely to influence sexual practices, holding a proportion of 16.1%, compared with 12.6% for parents. Friends were also more likely to be the first choice here (16.0% compared with 9.4%).

In the qualitative responses, participants often said that parents had not talked about sex with them, or had done so only fleetingly (Averett et al., 2009; Rahman and Jackson, 2010). Adam, a male heterosexual Christian said 'As a young teenage boy there is always the mates to talk to, sort of thing; they are the main avenues, certainly [it] wouldn't have been a parental strain of conversation, no'. While some parents refused to discuss sex, others used avoidance strategies such as using a book about reproduction as a replacement for conversations.

A minority of parents were very comfortable in talking about sex. Ellie said that she 'pretty much always had basic, age appropriate information . . . My parents have always been quite open'. Other parents who talked about sex channelled this through a discourse of danger. Layla, a heterosexual Muslim woman, explained that her mother had said, 'You know what boys [are like], they have got [the] sweet talk, they can literally make you drop your pants even if you're the strongest girl'. Vishaal concurred:

> *When I had my first girlfriend my mum absolutely laid into me about sex. She, like she sat me down for a good couple of hours and saying obviously giving me a big list about scripture and ethics and morality.*
> (Heterosexual Hindu man, interview)

Therefore it tended to be the case that when parents did discuss sex, sex was cast in dangerous terms, as something problematic and potentially damaging (Averett et al., 2009). In accordance with dominant discourses, boys were constructed as the source of danger, with girls cast as the victims of their advances (Johansson, 2007). Also of note is Vishaal's conceptualisation of the conversation in terms of religious ethics and morality. As Regnerus (2005) has outlined, religious parents are more likely to discuss morality than they are sex and contraception as the latter topics may be seen to encourage sexual behaviour.

When parents had not fostered open conversations about sexuality, participants often did not want to approach them with problems that arose. Some were hopeful that at some future point, parents could be utilised as a resource. Adala pondered exactly who she would approach if she encountered a sexual problem:

> *I think perhaps [I would] speak to my mum a little bit more about it . . . I think after I'm married, I think I would say to [my mother] that I've found it really, really hard to talk to you about it before . . . I'd explain to her, I'm happy I've got this husband and we're doing this. I think I'd go to the doctor. Obviously if it was a medical problem. I think I might discuss it with one of my friends.*

> (Heterosexual Muslim woman, interview)

Adala was waiting until marriage to become sexually active but her stream of consciousness was revealing. She started by saying that she would hope she could approach her mother for sexual advice once she was married, but then quickly backtracked, citing her doctor or friends as alternative ports of call. This shows that young adults do want satisfactory and honest relationships with their parents but feel uncomfortable at the prospect – for Adala, the idea that her mother could at some future point be her confidante quickly became untenable (Regnerus, 2007).

Friends were one of the most often utilised resources for talking about sex. Many participants found friends a great source of support in dealing with relationships, and indeed some reflected on their role in offering such support to their own friends in times of crisis, such as Sabrina who said 'My response is to be supportive and to listen to them and understand'. However, some male participants problematised their friendship networks:

> *If people are bragging about having had sex young you can feel, you know, less kind of comfortable with that . . . I don't have a group of guy mates that I will chat loads about sex with . . . when you're younger and you're less confident and you don't really know about [it].*

> (James, heterosexual Buddhist man, interview)

This quote illustrates potential high levels of misinformation and James's experience also tapped into the idea that men should automatically be knowledgeable experts. As Allen has argued, 'consulting friends risks masculine identity' (2005: 55).

However, friendships were diverse and multi-layered, with differences emerging along religious and cultural lines:

> *I might be in the pub with three un-churched . . . mates who will be talking about sex and things all evening and they would go into what they have been up to and it is an intriguing conversation. Or I could go into the pub with my church friends and we might talk about the issues but we wouldn't talk about the acts in depth, should we say. We might talk about the philosophical implications rather than the practical almost.*
>
> (Adam, heterosexual Christian man, interview)

> *[I would discuss sex with] all my close girlfriends, but not other girls that are Asian . . . if they asked me whether I was a virgin or not, I'd lie.*
>
> (Shalini, heterosexual Hindu woman, interview)

There could be a theory/practice split in the types of conversations young adults had with religious and non-religious friends. Some were reluctant to discuss sex with those of the same faith, particularly if one was having sex and this was against religious edicts (Sharma, 2011). Similarly, female participants who were remaining virgins until marriage could find that discussing this with their non-religious friends was problematic in a culture where there is little support for saving sex until marriage (McAndrew, 2010). Therefore, participants adapted to the friendship circle of the moment, following the norms for each group, displaying multiple selves, where knowledge and information would be concealed or repackaged depending on the situation.

Friends were also an important source of support for LGBT participants, who often told their friends first about their sexuality. Ryan, a homosexual Christian man, developed a non-religious circle of work friends who he told of his sexuality some time before he eventually told his parents. Erica, a lesbian who had attended a Jewish faith school, found her school friends an enormous source of support when she experienced hostility from others, saying 'I was so lucky with the group of friends'. This culminated when the school rabbis taught a class comparing homosexuality to bestiality, but Erica was supported through the experience by 'a lot of my friends who at the time were gay allies'.

Media

Compared with other sources of influence, the media scored quite low as participants' first choice, with 4.3% selecting this for the top response for influencing sexual values and attitudes, and 10.2% for influencing sexual practices. However, the internet, printed media or electronic media comprised 16.8% of the overall factors, going up to 21.1% in relation to influences on sexual practices. Therefore, there was a recognition that media has an impact, but it was often not considered a first choice for participants.

In the qualitative findings, participants discussed that the media was important in informing values and attitudes, but this was often underpinned by criticism too (Ashcraft, 2003). James saw certain films as glorifying losing one's virginity at the expense of sexual ethics:

> Modern films and stuff can be fairly awful . . . 'American Pie' . . . and there's like a big thing like 'Oh yeah we're going to lose our virginity' . . . which again are not really . . . I mean possibly realistic portrayals to some extent, but certainly not moral portrayals.

(Heterosexual Buddhist man, interview)

Therefore, similar to the ways in which participants divided their friendships into those from the same faith background where debates into morality and ethics could be had, and those with secular friends who discussed sexual practice, popular culture seemed to initiate the same divide. Magazines that distributed sex tips or films which portrayed seemingly vacuous sexual encounters were often viewed as not being underpinned by any ethical position. However, some participants were able to connect the two realms. Adala, a heterosexual Muslim woman, said that the storyline of the gay Muslim, Syed, in *Eastenders* had fostered discussion about homosexuality with her family, and she believed this was important so that 'people can be made aware'. Meanwhile, Jasmina, a heterosexual Muslim woman emphasised that the *Twilight* novels, where the key characters choose not to have sex before marriage, enabled her to 'talk about those kind of views, the views that I had about sex outside marriage to my friends who have different views and don't understand where I'm coming from'. Therefore, popular cultural scripts were utilised as springboards for broader ethical debate and discussion. In a context where religion is generally seen as outdated and holding an extremely conservative attitude about sex, connecting these two realms could allow participants to legitimise their own beliefs, and encourage broader understanding.

Concluding thoughts and some implications for practitioners

Participants felt that more discussion and debate about the practical, ethical and moral dimensions of sexuality was needed in faith contexts. Participants were very resourceful in carving out their own paths, but this could be difficult, especially when they were trying to mediate between seemingly non-negotiable rules presented in religious contexts, with forms of popular culture which could endorse sexual practices that were not connected with any discernible ethical position. Of course, this maps only a broad pattern and is not to suggest that these were either/or positions. As this chapter has shown, the reality is more complex than this.

Fostering discussion, however, was not the only issue. A related point was *how* this discussion was framed. While some participants were very supportive of being informed of firm rules around sexuality, for others, this approach was disliked, even making some think about whether they should remain within their faith tradition. Some participants did not want to even raise the debates they were wrestling with in religious contexts for fears of being judged or misheard. Safe spaces need to be created where young people can have honest and open discussion, discussion that highlights not just one theological viewpoint, but a broader spectrum.

Young adults now exist in a world where much emphasis is placed on individual reasoning about what one believes (Bragg and Buckingham, 2009; Savage et al., 2006). Young people are situated as knowing subjects, who articulate their desires in a context of choice. Consumerist rhetoric has infused much of everyday life, not only in terms of what consumer goods are purchased but also in terms of beliefs and attitudes. In this mixed market place, choice is privileged so long as harm is not induced. Reflexivity and negotiation replaces diktats and rule-following. Rather than authoritative relationships being normative (e.g. between parents and children, teachers and pupils, religious leaders and religious adherents), this has been displaced with a more indefinite power structure. Parents negotiate respect with their children. Teachers earn their respect over a period of time. Authority structures are not simply accepted and absorbed. So when young people hear certain pronouncements and edicts from religious leaders, these will not be simply supported and endorsed. Rather, young people expect a period of negotiation and discussion – as happens in other spheres of their life.

The participants in this research were keen to assert themselves as active agents in the process of learning about sexuality and working out their own ethical position. Bragg and Buckingham have highlighted how young people rely heavily on media outlets to inform their views about sexuality, with a variety of scripts being considered in order to make up one's mind. Religious viewpoints become one among many, alongside the plethora of options available, and religions are not necessarily doing a good job at either disseminating a religious viewpoint or cultivating this in an environment where young people feel they are making up their own minds. Religions are well-positioned to give young people what they want – an ethically-grounded approach to sexuality. As Smith and Denton's research on religion among American youth articulated, young people have certain values they uphold such as human rights, dignity and equality, but they have 'few coherent, rational grounds for explaining, justifying and defending those standards' (2005: 96). For our participants, religion was seen as a crucial site where one's ethics could be worked out, but as already indicated, a number of participants felt a gap in the knowledges being presented between secular and religious cultures, and they had to be resourceful in bridging this gap themselves. The practicalities of sex were not often issues on the agenda and neither were there many concrete opportunities for sexual ethics to be debated. But tensions arise when young adults' beliefs (e.g. around homosexuality) are out of synch with faith leaders (Yip and Page, 2013). As Regnerus (2007) asserts, a conservative line may be taken by religious leaders on issues such as sex outside of marriage and homosexuality but this may be at odds with discourses in the media and education system. Young people may subscribe to more conservative views of sexuality but equally they may subscribe to liberal interpretations. Others remain undecided. What is clear is that religions are seen in sex-negative terms in the broader context (Plummer, 2003; Weeks, 2007). Significantly, if self-identified religious youth are struggling with these issues, then there will be little appeal to those outside the religious framework who will continue to view religious spaces as intolerant and repressive.

Youth workers and religious leaders can foster debate with young people; creating spaces where opinions can be freely shared, questions can be raised, perhaps initiated by current affairs or examples from popular culture (Savage et al., 2006). But crucially this has to be undertaken in a non-judgemental fashion, where young people's thoughts are valued and heard, and where a variety of theological interpretations are offered. Otherwise, didactic styles will continue to appeal to an ever-smaller number of young people.

References

Allen, L. (2005) *Sexual Subjects*. Basingstoke: Palgrave Macmillan.

Ashcraft, C. (2003) Adolescent Ambiguities in American Pie. *Youth and Society*, 35: 1, 37–70.

Averett, P., Benson, M. and Vaillancourt, K. (2009) Young Women's Struggle for Sexual Agency. *Journal of Gender Studies*, 17: 4, 331–44.

Bragg, S. and Buckingham, D. (2009) Too Much Too Young? In Attwood, F. (Ed.) *Mainstreaming Sex*. London: I.B. Tauris.

Coleman, L.M. and Testa, A. (2008) Sexual Health Knowledge, Attitudes and Behaviours UK. *Ethnicity and Health*, 13: 1, 55–72.

Cooksey, E. and Dooms, T. (2010) The Role of Religion in the Sexual Lives of Teens. In Collins-Mayo, S. and Dandelion, P. (Eds.) *Religion and Youth*. Farnham: Ashgate.

Durham, M.G. (2002) Girls, Media, and the Negotiation of Sexuality. In Williams, C.L. and Stein, A. (Eds.) *Sexuality and Gender*. Oxford: Blackwell.

Elias, N. (1982) *The Civilizing Process*. Oxford: Blackwell.

Epstein, D., O'Flynn, S. and Telford, D.L. (2003) *Silenced Sexualities in Schools and Universities*. Stoke on Trent: Trentham Books.

Freitas, D. (2008) *Sex and the Soul*. Oxford: Oxford University Press.

Johansson, T. (2007) *The Transformation of Sexuality*. Aldershot: Ashgate.

Kehily, M.J. (2002) *Sexuality, Gender and Schooling*. London: Routledge.

McAndrew, S. (2010) Religious Faith and Contemporary Attitudes. In Park, A. et al., (Eds.) *British Social Attitudes: The 26th Report*. London: Sage.

Plummer, K. (2003) *Intimate Citizenship: Private Decisions and Public Dialogue*. Montreal: McGill-Queen's University Press.

Rahman, M. and Jackson, S. (2010) *Gender and Sexuality*. Cambridge: Polity Press.

Regnerus, M.D. (2005) Talking about Sex. *The Sociological Quarterly*, 46: 1, 79–105.

Regnerus, M.D. (2007) *Forbidden Fruit*. Oxford: Oxford University Press.

Savage, S., Collins-Mayo, S., Mayo, B. and Cray, G. (2006) *Making Sense of Generation Y: The World View of 15–25-Year-olds*. London: Church House Publishing.

Sharma, S. (2011) *Good Girls, Good Sex*. Halifax and Winnipeg: Fernwood Publishing.

Smith, C. and Denton, M.L. (2005) *Soul Searching: The Religious and Spiritual Lives of American Teenagers*. New York: Oxford University Press.

Weeks, J. (2007) *The World We Have Won: The Remaking of Erotic and Intimate Life*. Abingdon: Routledge.

Yip, A.K.T. and Page, S. (2013) *Religious and Sexual Identities: A Multi-faith Exploration of Young Adults*. Farnham: Ashgate.

CHAPTER 7

Youth Work, Faith, Values and Indoctrination

Pete Harris

> *There is a legitimate concern that workers who have a religious allegiance may use opportunities that arise in their work as human services {op. cit} practitioners to seek to persuade vulnerable people to adopt their . . . religious points of view.*
>
> (Moss, 2005: 21)

> *There are a worrying number of books that operate from a non-dia-logical basis. That is to say, their writers are neither generally willing to entertain that their knowledge . . . may be flawed or wrong.*
>
> (Doyle and Smith, 2014: web)

Should youth workers promote their own values when these are based on a personal religious faith or should they remain neutral and operate in such a way so that young people are free to make up their own minds? This chapter attempts to set that question in a British youth and community work context and examine the relationship between the notions which lie at the heart of it – faith, values and indoctrination.

At the outset, it is worth clarifying that the term faith is being used here to refer to religious faith of all kinds found in the UK, including Christian, Muslim, Buddhist, Hindu, Sikh, etc., although the argument developed seeks to highlight similarities between religious and secular worldviews. It is also worth acknowledging that two key assumptions underlie the position developed herein: firstly, that young people do not (and cannot) acquire values entirely independently of adults or their peers – they can (and do) learn them from both; and, secondly, that youth work's purpose (at least in part) should be to contribute to a more just and healthy society. On that basis, this chapter will:

- examine the concept of values, drawing a distinction between those which have an ethical, moral basis and those which do not;

- examine first the relationship between religious belief and values and then youth work and values, arguing value neutrality is neither possible nor desirable within a youth work context;
- clarify what is, and is not, indoctrination, and suggest that the greatest protection against indoctrination is to maintain a dialogical approach to youth work practice;
- identify a way forward for youth work practice and some lessons for youth work training programmes in the UK.

Values – moral and non-moral

So, what do we mean by values? According to Moss (2007: 1) 'At its simplest, a value is something we hold dear, something we see as important and worthy of safeguarding'. However, we need to be clear as to what we mean when we say we 'value' certain things. We may value concrete things or physical objects, like a car or house. They are prized and important to us. But other things we value are more abstract, like tolerance or compassion; or they may be expressed as personal qualities – things that people can be, or fail to be (e.g. tolerant or compassionate) – or as rules (e.g. don't tell lies).

Graham Haydon (1997: 34) draws a useful distinction between what he calls 'non-moral' values and 'moral' values. Saying that somebody's belief in horoscopes is wrong, may only be to question its factual truth, which is different to saying that believing in horoscopes is morally wrong. There is a difference between advising a young person to listen to classical music rather than pop music because classical music may have *aesthetic* value and advising them that they *should* not listen to pop music because of *unethical* lyrical content. Conflict most often arises when our values become things that we think others *should* adopt. The focus here will be on this type of value, what Haydon calls moral values – i.e. those with an ethical dimension, such as 'it is wrong to have sex before marriage'. These are the values that often create the most debate and dissention, and pose thorny dilemmas for youth workers around whether they should seek to persuade young people to adopt these values too.

Religious belief and moral values

It is conceivable for someone to believe there is life on other planets and for another person to believe there is not. Neither can prove their assertion, although they may seek to marshal supporting evidence. It would be unusual, though, for a discussion between the believer and non-believer in this case to escalate into violence. Religious faith usually involves a deeply held set of beliefs (such as in the existence of a divine being or in reincarnation). These beliefs may amount to commands from God to be obeyed unquestioningly, or represent the basis of an ongoing dialogue or a process of emergent understanding through revelation. For the religious believer, believing that an act is against the divine order of things may be sufficient to make it ethically wrong.

In turn, the religious believer's values (what they see as important and worth safeguarding) may be informed and strengthened by their beliefs. Faith provides the overarching meaning in which these values are situated. Values begin to define people and become part of their identity. Difficulties come about when the road divides between 'secular' values and traditional religious values around, say, sex and sexuality. The question then arises as to whether secular values, supposedly rooted in reason and rationality, have in themselves more value than so called religious values which, being based on beliefs and faith, can be seen as inherently irrational. However, this question is not resolvable in those terms because the 'truth' of moral values cannot be objectively established in the same way as the factual truth of science or mathematics. Whilst it could be a fact that I value sexual chastity (subjectively), it is not a fact that sexual chastity has value (objectively). Values are not states of affairs in the physical world.

Youth work and values

Because values grounded in a religious faith can come to define a culture and provide a sense of belonging, any threat to those values can be experienced as intimidating and a potent source of conflict. The presence of conflicting value systems in close proximity over time can become increasingly problematic. For some, this leads to the conclusion that communities with different value systems should lead separate lives. When in a minority, or surrounded by others with a different value base, life can feel lonely and threatening. Youth workers can often end up working with young people in that lonely and threatening space, both physically and psychologically. If workers want to avoid conflict, they may see their role as preparing young people for a world with a plurality of values, and where difference is celebrated and valued in itself. This is partly reflected in the inclusion until recently, of 'spiritual' development as a separate standard within the National Occupational Standards for Youth Work in the UK.

This standard is about working with young people to explore ethical, moral and cultural values, addressing the need to respect the beliefs and values of others. It includes exploring where young people are on their journeys through life and encouraging them to see themselves in terms of their relationships with others and the environment around them.

(Lifelong Learning UK, 2008: 1.1.4)

Whilst it has since been removed as a separate standard, it is still recognised as an aspect of youth work. In the UK then, there is already a clear expectation that youth workers will engage in activities with young people that challenge them to explore and develop a sense of their own and others' beliefs and values. Processes of 'values clarification' (Kirschenbaum and Simon, 1973) can be seen as part of that effort. Here we are dealing with attempts made to simply make the implicit explicit, to reveal to young people what values they already hold and why, so as to bring those values under greater critical control. Although value clarification is a useful and often powerful exercise when working with young people, it masks more fundamental realities that, if we fail to recognise them, will confuse our thinking in this area. Such a position seems to take a neutral stance on values development. Young people are enabled simply to understand themselves better – what answers they arrive at remains at their discretion. According to this view, educators should not therefore express a view or seek to 'influence'.

But any process that seeks to engender in children and young people the values of, for example, telling the truth, keeping promises, tolerance, fairness, listening and respect (which in turn lay the bedrock for democratic debate, dialogue and the development of autonomy) is one which the child does not necessarily choose to adopt. We as parents, carers and educators will often make that choice for them in what we decide is in their (and society's) interest. All *socialisation* processes (assuming we are seeking to develop desirable habits of conduct) require the parent, carer, teacher or worker to present these as desirable. We can present them as possibilities rather than a *fait accompli*, but with young children this still inevitably requires, amongst a range of approaches, the use of behaviourist methods of reward and punishment and role modelling until powers of reasoning are sufficiently developed to allow more autonomous decision-making. Any parent will confirm that the enterprise of moulding or forming a child into a socialised adult sometimes requires elements of a behaviourist approach and a small child in particular may not be given a choice, or be fully able to understand the reason for his/her parents' decisions. The use of a degree of adult power to instil a sense of value within this scenario is unavoidable. This creation of a 'primary culture' is necessary to provide a coherent structure from which the child can understand the world and develop capacity for moral reasoning in the future. It is of course, not the same as an educative process, at least as youth workers would understand it. The youth worker's role when working with teenagers is to both build on this basis whilst at the same time developing young people's ability to autonomously critique that primary culture.

The idea that those working with young people can somehow be neutral when it comes to values quickly evaporates on even a cursory analysis. The key values believed to underpin youth work are clearly articulated in the National Occupational Standards and taught (indeed promoted) on current training courses. These standards represent the outcome of the profession coming together to agree a set of values. Others (e.g. Merton and Wylie, 2005) have promoted the creation of a youth work curriculum – which has inherent within it the notion that that we *should* value certain educational outcomes. Furthermore, the radical perspective of so-called 'de-schoolers' such as Ivan Illich (1977) reminds us that the existence of a 'profession' itself suggests that we value the placing of 'professional' adults alongside young people – and prompts us to question the value of that in itself. How professionalism is conceived within youth work and whether youth work can be considered a profession at all, remains hotly contested (Koehn,1994). Traditional models of professionalism which assume a dispassionate distance between professional worker and young person do not sit easily with conceptions of the youth worker as an informal and moral educator (Young, 1999).

Despite this, youth workers in the UK (at least in theory) are conceived as professionally trained workers who seek to educate young people in such a way as is of value to society as a whole as well as the individual. State funded youth work has, to a large extent, set out its stall in this regard. Youth work as a profession in the UK does not currently and has never worked on the basis that moral values are entirely relative or merely about subjective personal preference. If it did, entering into debates about values with young people would have no purpose beyond that of entertainment or the aesthetic pleasure that that debate brought about. As citizens, we may feel that some matters should be about personal choice – e.g. sexual behaviour – and choose to attach no morality to it. But youth work does not do this in all cases, such as those involving child abuse or oppression. If a young person with learning difficulties was being bullied within a project, are there any conceivable circumstances where a worker would consider it appropriate to not intervene or express a view – or, at the very least, to intervene in such a way as to encourage young people to articulate the basis of their actions? Although conceptions of the 'good' may differ, workers are generally encouraged to aim for the 'good' of both the individual and the good of society as part of their stated purpose. As such this precludes the idea of value 'neutrality'. In reality we need to acknowledge that professional youth work values are such that there is no ambiguity or relativity around certain values. Workers are not expected to remain non-directive or neutral on such matters as injustice, discrimination and oppression or unethical and abusive behaviour.

Huge emphasis is placed within the youth work discourse on creating environments where young people can learn to make their own decisions. The desire of the worker to respect the autonomy of young people and, at the same time, the needs of the wider community, is in itself a choice based on values. Stressing the need for a young person to make free choice as to his or her values or encouraging young people to question their beliefs involves inculcation of that questioning as valuable in itself (presumably without the young person's permission). There is therefore a fundamental paradox within any notion of non-directive, neutral value clarification. This is a 'worldview' too – a way of looking at the world. As such it could also be viewed as a form of primary culture that therefore has the potential to be culturally specific too. By virtue of living in Western society, we unconsciously adhere to certain legal, ethical and philosophical positions that are grounded in liberal democratic viewpoints (e.g. notions of Rawlsian procedural justice, individualism, freedom, etc.); market and consumerist ideologies; and faith traditions that we have not freely chosen. In fact some of these notions we consider our 'gospel' and as the grounds for our professional practice as youth workers (such as democracy and autonomy) are viewed and experienced entirely differently by other cultures.

Perhaps most pertinently, whether driven by a religious faith or other secular worldviews, workers may also feel it is legitimate as part of their professional activity to seek to persuade young people that certain values should take precedence over others; for example, criticality and creativity over materialistic consumption (Smith, 1982). Moreover, some conflict between people due to opposing values could be viewed as positive because of its potential to lead to progress and change, as with the abolition of slavery or the enfranchisement of women. Change such as this arises because of the presence of a vocal minority that seek to change the status quo, sometimes through violence (e.g. freedom fighters in South Africa).

Indoctrination and dialogical practice

So what of the concern that 'workers may use opportunities that arise in their work as human services . . . practitioners to seek to persuade vulnerable people to adopt their [worker's] religious points of view' (Moss, 2005: 21)? Is there a heightened risk of indoctrination if workers allow their own faith-based values to encroach on their practice? How is one to distinguish the indoctrinator from the one who seeks to persuade and influence others to value certain things?

R.S. Peters (1973: 71) defines indoctrination as 'getting children to accept a fixed body of rules by the use of techniques which incapacitate them from adopting a critical autonomous attitude toward them'. Similarly, Michael Taylor (1985: 25) claims that 'indoctrination interferes with the ability to be self-determining with regard to beliefs and judgments'.

The indoctrinated mind then, is one that is not open to alternatives and will not engage in dialogue to justify its own values and beliefs. It has been hoodwinked or deceived into believing and valuing only what the indoctrinator wants it to believe and value, and has no control over that process.

This process is in stark contrast to the educational and youth work ideals of democracy, open-mindedness, rationality, critical thinking, autonomy and dialogue. Through dialogue, as Socrates argued, we move closer to truth. Dialogue can be understood as a form of *truth-seeking* where both worker and young people identify themselves as learners as well as educators and are continually ready to join with the other in exploration, with a preparedness to change their own thinking. To work with young people so they stop struggling and thinking would be the essence of indoctrinatory (and non-dialogical) practice.

Haydon argues that there is a distinction to be drawn between the religious and non-religious person.

> *The secular moralist, aware of how much people can differ in their values, may always maintain some room for the thought that others may be right after all. But the believer who has a quite unshakeable religious faith may by the same token have the strongest possible conviction of the correctness of certain moral positions.*
>
> (Haydon, 1997: 47)

Presumably Haydon is referring to the religious believer. But could not atheists be similarly committed to their non-belief in God and similarly passionate that others should subscribe to their beliefs and values? Is it not possible to be a fundamentalist, evangelical atheist (*a la* Richard Dawkins, 2007)? Do we not all seek to persuade and influence others to adopt our own perspective or values to some degree? The more pressing issue is how we use our power and authority over others, particularly over those who may be overly susceptible to influence. Religious believers may include fundamentalists but it does not follow that subscribing to a religious faith precludes doubt and therefore dialogue. Any fanatic (according to Christian existentialist theologian, Paul Tillich) replaces doubt with certainty because of the existential angst lurking beneath the surface of the psyche.

> *He flees from his freedom of asking and answering for himself to a situation in which no further questions can be asked and the answers to previous questions are imposed on him authoritatively. In order to avoid the risk of asking and doubting, he surrenders the right to ask and doubt.*

(Tillich, 1952: 56)

Organised religion may have a violent and conflict-ridden past but there is nothing inherent in a belief in God that prevents the acknowledgment of different or opposing beliefs in others, any more than a belief in the non-existence of God. Furthermore, there is no reason for the history of religious intransience and intolerance to dictate the present or future. A more likely explanation of such intolerance is the role that religious belief plays in the behaviour of those who are living in polarised or deprived and oppressed communities and the way religious belief can become a hook to hang ones grievances against the 'other' (Said, 1978). Where religious communities are located in countries where some plurality of values is tolerated, we can often observe a greater degree of what Haydon terms 'cross fertilisation' (1997: 47) i.e. a process by which different values come to influence the religions practiced within that culture.

Atheistic and politically committed practitioners cannot claim to be acting in an entirely non-directive way. To question the legitimacy of work infused with faith-based values and yet strongly defend the right of workers to engage in political education is, at the least, problematic if not contradictory. Seeking to engage young people in existential questions such as the search for meaning and purpose, or even to promote what might more accurately be called 'spiritual' or values such as peace, forgiveness, sacrifice, hope, human connectedness, is arguably as equally valid as the promotion of such values as trust, respect, collectivity, civic courage, perseverance, and open-mindedness.

At times within professional debate, it appears that whereas these secular values are viewed as entirely appropriate, those that may emerge from a faith-based or spiritual worldview are not – presumably because these faith-based values are themselves, valued less.

It is of course important for individuals to be clear about their own values and the significance they have for them because without this kind of under-standing dialogue is not possible. But, as we have seen, seemingly neutral notions of value clarification are in fact value laden (i.e. it is 'good' to clarify your values). Can one consistently espouse the need to criticise and ques-tion certain moral values and yet at the same time espouse unquestioningly others? For example, as workers we unquestioningly defend the idea of democracy as 'good' in comparison with anarchy, despotism, etc., and seek to foster the valuing of it through experience. In our defence of democratic education, is it possible that some workers are in danger of taking a less than dialogical approach to that debate and even seeking to indoctrinate others into their own worldview?

A way forward for youth work practice

Young people need opportunities to make choices about their values and they cannot do this without engaging in dialogue. Workers can seek to promote certain values and work in non-indoctrinatory ways as long as they conceive of themselves as *truth seekers* rather than *truth holders* seeking to win an argument. Dialogue is only possible, however, if we state what we value and believe to be true at that time and then seek to understand what the other values and sees as true, likewise, at that time. Dialogue does not mean that we should not share what we value with young people or engage in some kind of descent into moral relativism. The process of declaring your values, convictions and beliefs does not become indoctrination as long as it is accom-panied by a commitment to listen to and learn from the values, convictions and beliefs of others. In the Socratic dialogical tradition, it is this process, including even the juxtaposition of 'true' and 'false' that has value in itself and enables us all to develop. Workers are not engaged in indoctrination when they state what they personally believe in and value, even when these beliefs and values entail a moral, ethical or spiritual dimension.

The perceived tension between youth work and faith is borne out of a nervousness around the exclusive claims to truth posited by certain members of faith groups. It is undeniable that in many parts of the world and through-out history, such a non-dialogical approach to truth has led to violence and injustice on a global scale. Workers who are members of faith groups, make exclusive claims for the Quran or the Bible, deny that there may be truth in anything other than their own tradition and seek to convince young people to believe the same, are operating in opposition to youth work principles. Work with young people in any religious faith context that seeks to evangelise and convert young people needs to be recognised as an activity that those with such convictions can legitimately seek to do, but must be distinguished from education and youth work. Blind disregard for professional principles and a refusal to engage with matters that cause doubt or inner conflict, or an excessively judgmental approach to young people has no place within the profession. In this sense, it may be that we need to be employ a further paradox, the 'paradox of tolerance'.

> *Unlimited tolerance must lead to the disappearance of tolerance. If we extend unlimited tolerance even to those who are intolerant, if we are not prepared to defend a tolerant society against the onslaught of the intolerant, then the tolerant will be destroyed, and tolerance with them.*

(Popper, 1945: Chapter 7, note 4)

The problem with not tolerating intolerance, of course, is that some young people that workers engage with are exactly that – intolerant. Young people who have, often through the indoctrinatory activities of others, come to have sympathy with fascist politics or religious violent extremism can pose a stern challenge to democratically minded practitioners. In this context, youth workers' intolerance should not equate to a refusal to engage with young people with such beliefs and values. It is through meaningful dialogue with these young people that change becomes possible. Such dialogue involves the use of both powers of reason and influence, to confront irrational beliefs as well as inter and intra-faith dialogue (i.e. between and within faith communities) around how sacred texts are interpreted and understood. Relationship and rapport-building skills remain key if workers are to get alongside these young people and bring their influence to bear. In the face of such a challenge, faith in God or simply the underlying potential of young people, or the goodness of human nature, is at times invaluable as a motivating and sustaining force.

There is a long tradition of faith-based work that respects the emphasis on autonomy inherent in youth work (Milson, 1963) and many educators with a personal faith would be anxious to avoid indoctrination (Tan, 2003). Atheistic practitioners with strongly held political convictions or with a strong commitment to a particular worldview (could we say even a 'faith' in an ideology such as communism, socialism, feminism or anarchism?) should be equally anxious too. Any pedagogy, whether faith-based or politically-based, that seeks to inculcate the same and uncritical worldview in others through the use of power, particularly with young people whose relatively restricted levels of awareness and experience could leave them overly vulnerable to influence, could quite rightly be described as indoctrination. Matters of religious faith seen in this light therefore become irrelevant to this discussion. It is dialogical practice that is key and offers the best protection against indoctrination of whatever sort. Clearly, where young people are particularly vulnerable to suggestion and influence, workers need to be vigilant as to how they are exerting their influence. But in most cases, the chance of youth workers indoctrinating young people is actually quite low, particularly in the context of all the other influences in young peoples' lives. Young people (more so than young children) can choose to adopt values as their own and still retain the ability to defend their view and think about its limits. A young person choosing to commit to a religious faith or to become involved in political or protest movements does not automatically imply they have been indoctrinated. Denying young people the chance to be exposed to political, religious or spiritual values out of a desire to avoid influencing young people, takes away from them the opportunity to make autonomous choices about their beliefs and values.

If we revisit our definition of indoctrination as the inability of the young person to be critical, justify their values or be open to alternatives, then as long as workers engage in dialogue, are clear about the possibility of alternative viewpoints, encourage young people to articulate the basis of their values and do so themselves, they are not denying young people autonomy. It is also possible to seek to exert influence around certain values whilst, at the same time promoting a critical awareness too. We may seek in Western democratic states to promote liberal values (or from a faith perspective, certain spiritual values) whilst also developing awareness that other cultures may emphasise other values. Youth and community projects and clubs provide fertile environments for this debate as young people from different backgrounds encounter different political and cultural value systems. In essence, we need to equip young people with the critical capacity to question and develop their values. This process of joint truth seeking has the capacity to bring people together, not divide them. Attempting to break down barriers between communities does not require us to first abandon our own truth and traditions, rather a commitment to understand them more fully, followed by a commitment to learning from the truth and tradition of others.

Lessons for youth work training

For youth workers in training, what is required is a similar space for the development and critical appraisal of the socialised self. For sure, the profession demands adherence to a set of professional values and in certain areas these could come into conflict with deeply held personal convictions. Becoming aware that others hold different views and that (more importantly) certain views are considered 'unprofessional' can lead to the suppression of those views. For workers, this could mean they simply seep out later in practice. Where personal or communal beliefs and values clash with professional values, simply burying them and concealing this struggle from young people has limited educational value, dilutes authenticity in the relationship and can leave workers feeling paralysed. An approach that allows exploration of these convictions with an expressed value of openness to others (indeed, as a professional expectation) should pave the way for effective teamwork and more productive personal and professional relationships. Students should be encouraged to explore each other's journey and examine the foundations for the differences that inevitably arise. All meaningful dialogue starts with and is enriched by a level of self-awareness. Time to reflect with others both, of a similar and dissimilar mind, within a faith community can, when facilitated in a 'safe space', produce a more developmental dialogue with those who have a different perspective. By encouraging deeper reflection on one's own journey, the ability to imagine the journey of others is increased, not deterred.

The student who better understands why he/she believes what he/she does is better placed to understand why others feel the way they do and may also be better placed to make changes to that belief system if it no longer meets his/her needs. In order to detach oneself from socialisation and become more autonomous, the shared experience of discussing how this socialisation occurred eases the process of critique.

In summary

The relationship between youth work, faith, values and indoctrination requires careful thought and not just a knee jerk response. Here we have focused on faith in its religious manifestation, but faith – if in nothing else, then in young people themselves – that they can be more than they may be when we first encounter them – lies at the heart of secular youth work too. Faith in the possibility of human progress motivates many workers with either a religious or political worldview and abandoning any discourse of such faith weakens the potential power of our work. Working towards the 'common good' and the alleviation of at least some of the social problems we face in society requires more than legislation and values clarification. It requires a value and moral transformation – a 'change in hearts and minds' (Sandel, 2010: 245).

Society's greatest reformers were often motivated by faith. Religions by no means have the monopoly on attempts to indoctrinate the young.

Youth work, at its best has a strong sense of purpose and the common good. Definitions of what 'good' and 'human flourishing' mean within a youth work context have long been, and continue to be, discussed (Jeffs and Smith, 1990). To detach ourselves from that aspiration would be to impoverish our discourse. Youth workers cannot and should not avoid moral values. Such an approach does not prepare young people for the reality of diversity. An absence of values – or a vacuum – will be filled with the prevailing hegemonic value system in society. Faith, in all its guises including the religious, can give a sense of meaning and hope to young people – particularly in a world that increasingly values the 'wrong' things (e.g. materialism, celebrity, consumption and unbridled individualism). Good workers have strong convictions and seek to cultivate values in young people, which could include those of a *spiritual* if not exclusively religious hue such as, compassion, mature love, fellowship or being able to see the universal significance of events. Strong religious convictions do not preclude tolerance and dialogue; and dialogue does not require neutrality or impartiality. Where disagreements arise we can be central to the process of increasing understanding and mutual respect. Value judgements have a place in society – however diverse – and in youth work. Faith-based youth work that seeks to work with young people so they come to value solidarity, mutual responsibility, tolerance, compassion, forgiveness, commitment to social justice, etc., shares a deep commonality with 'secular' youth work that seeks to do the same, as long as it is critical and dialogical in its nature.

If both young people and workers are encouraged to take an active part in their learning; if learning relationships are structured to create dialogue and critical engagement, and to enable young people and workers to delve into their own systems of meaning then there is both clear commonality between the two and an opportunity for real transformative practice. The real tragedy lies in the fact that far too often this commonality is lost within an academic and professional debate that is based on flawed philosophical thinking.

References

Dawkins, R. (2007) *The God Delusion*. London: Black Swan.

Doyle, M. E. and Smith M. K. (1999) *Born and Bred? Leadership, Heart and Informal Education*. London: The Rank Foundation/YMCA George Williams College.

Doyle, M. E. and Smith, M. K. (2014) Christian Youth Work (youthwork) – A Guide to Reading. *The encylopaedia of informal education*. http://www.infed.org/youthwork/b-ywchri.htm

Haydon, G. (1997) *Teaching About Values, A New Approach*. London: Cassell.

Illich, I. (1977) *Disabling Professions*. London: Marion Boyars.

Jeffs, T. and Smith, M. (1990) *Using Informal Education: An Alternative to Casework, Teaching, and Control?* Milton Keynes: Open University Press.

Kirschenbaum, H. and Simon, S. B. (1973) *Readings in Values Clarification*. Minneapolis: Winston Press.

Koehn, D. (1994) *The Ground of Professional Ethics*. London: Routledge.

Lifelong Learning UK (2008) *National Occupational Standards for Youth Work/*. London: Lifelong Learning UK.

Merton, B. and Wylie, T. (2002) *Towards a Contemporary Youth Work Curriculum*. Leicester: National Youth Agency.

Milson, F.W. (1963) *Social Group Method and Christian Education*. London: Chester House Publications.

Moss, B. (2005) *Religion and Spirituality*. Lyme Regis: Russell House.

Moss, B. (2007) *Values*. Lyme Regis: Russell House.

Peters, R. S. (1973) *Reason and Compassion*. London: Routledge and Kegan Paul.

Popper, K. R. (1945) *The Open Society and its Enemies*. London: Routledge & Sons Ltd.

Pugh, C. (1999) Christian Youth Work: Evangelism or Social Action. *The encylopaedia of informal education*. http://www.infed.org/christianeducation/christianyw.htm.

Radcliffe, T. (2005) *What is the Point in Being a Christian?* London: Burns and Oates.

Said, E. (1978) *Orientalism*. New York: Pantheon Books.

Sandel, M. J. (2010) *Justice. What's the Right Thing to do?* London: Penguin.

Smith, M. (1982) *Creators not Consumers. Rediscovering Social Education*. Leicester: NAYC Publications.

Smith, M. (2005) Christian Youth Work: A Guide to Reading. *The encyclopaedia of informal education*. [http://www.infed.org/youthwork/b-ywchri.htm. Retrieved: March 2012].

Tan, C. (2003) Christian Education Without the Problem of Indoctrination. *Quodlibet Journal*, 5: 4. [http://www.quodlibet.net/articles/tan-education.shtml. Retrieved: October 2, 2014]

Taylor, M. (1985) Children and Other Barbarians. *Southwest Philosophy Review*, 2: 19–24.

Tillich, P (1952) *The Courage to Be*. London: Fontana.

Young, K (1999) *The Art of Youth Work*. Lyme Regis: Russell House.

CHAPTER 8

Finding a Middle Way Between Faith-based and Secular Youth and Community Work Courses

Helen Bardy, Pauline Grace, Pete Harris, John Holmes, Mike Seal

With the notable growth of faith-based youth provision and the consequent growth of faith-based higher education national qualifying (JNC) courses in Youth and Community Work over the last fifteen years, it might have been expected that this would have influenced the curriculum of the majority of courses based on secular principles. This does not appear to have been the case. Rather there has been a resistance by secular courses to accept faith as part of the core curriculum. Equally, although faith-based courses have drawn on the body of knowledge developed by secular courses, there are clear indications that the faith-based courses may want to increasingly find a separate path.

This chapter argues that this division between faith-based and secular is unhelpful to the education of Youth and Community workers, and there is a need to bring together not only students from different faiths but also those with no religious faith to engage in open ended dialogue about their values, and the place of faith and spirituality in Youth and Community Work. We draw on our work at Newman University in Birmingham where, since 2007, we have run optional pathways for both Christian and Muslim students. Students on these pathways are integrated with a larger student group that is studying Youth and Community Work from a secular perspective. This diversity of faith is also reflected in the current staff team at Newman University who represent a range of personal views on religious faith (Roman Catholic, Muslim, agnostic, communist/atheist).

The Newman experience acts as a case study for the identification of the important elements of a training strategy for youth workers that encourages dialogue between workers of differing values and traditions. This is particularly crucial in the current context where much statutory provision has been taken over by voluntary or faith-based providers, and where youth workers of all backgrounds may find themselves working alongside, or even for, faith-based organisations. As far as we are aware, the Newman course is the only British JNC qualifying course that explicitly aims to bring together youth work practitioners of different faith and non-faith backgrounds, with a curriculum plan to promote critical and respectful dialogue. We believe it is essential that all JNC qualifying courses recognise the reality of British society and the pivotal role that religious faith plays, and have curriculum strategies to respond to this situation.

Historical developments

There has been significant growth in the last fifteen years of JNC qualifying courses linked to the faith sector (the Institute for Children, Youth and Mission – now with centres in Bristol, Cambridge, Ireland, Midlands and Oxford; Moorlands College – Christchurch; Oasis College, London; Nazarene College, Manchester; International Christian College, Glasgow; University of Chester; Newman University, Birmingham). According to NYA figures from the 2010–11 annual monitoring survey of English courses there were 3,276 people undertaking JNC qualifying courses, of which 269 were from faith-based courses representing 8.2% or about 1 in 12 of the total group (Evans, 2012). Most of these courses are Christian and evangelical, differing from the Newman course which includes other Christian approaches, notably Roman Catholic (reflecting the mission of Newman University) as well as other religious faiths (notably Muslim, reflecting the demographics of the West Midlands).

The origins of youth work in the nineteenth century are clearly from Judaeo-Christian roots and the diverse voluntary sector has maintained links to particular denominations (e.g. The Children's Society and the Church of England) or to a broader belief in the importance of religious faith (e.g. The Scouts). However, the development of a professional youth service linked to the Welfare State post 1945 was on a secular basis and so the initial JNC courses, which emerged after the 1960 Albemarle Report, were established as such. There were some crossovers with courses such as Westhill College in Birmingham, with its Methodist roots, and the YMCA George Williams College in London. However, in courses such as these the links to faith organisations weakened and a curriculum with a faith emphasis increasingly declined, although some Christian students were still attracted because of the faith origins of these colleges.

The growth of faith-based JNC courses in the last fifteen years could be viewed as an effect of the voluntary sector seeking to professionalise as it grew in strength. It might also be viewed as a response to a gap in the market, with students from largely secular courses being seen by faith-based employers as insufficiently prepared around faith matters. Employers of all kinds have often made calls to change the structure and approach to courses. Over the last thirty years there have been a number of employer led initiatives to promote part time or apprentice type courses for Youth Service employees. Alongside this, the government (and government-funded agencies such as the NYA) have promoted the interests of employers over other interest groups (such as young people's groups, workers' bodies, academic lecturers, or the students themselves). However, many of these part time and apprentice type initiatives were short lived, as the funding dried up or the initial cohorts became qualified. Some courses became incorporated into other HE courses, and the part time route to qualification became common. Arguably, it is time to be equally responsive to the growing faith sector.

Even before current cutbacks hit local authority Youth Services, it was claimed that Christian churches were the largest employers of youth workers, at 5,500 fte more than the statutory sector (Brierley, 2003). Although such statistical measures will always face the perennial difficulty of defining what actually constitutes youth work, it is clear that there has been a revival in Christian based youth work. Doyle and Smith (2002; 2013) argue that the recent history of British Christian youth ministry has yet to be written. It seems clear, however, that the recent growth partly reflects concerns about the ageing membership of some Christian denominations and partly the revival of increasingly socially concerned Christian, often evangelical agencies, which is a reflection of trends elsewhere in the world (notably the USA – see Infed, ud.). The development of distinct faith-based, initially Christian, professional qualifying courses in youth work came about through concerns from Christian agencies recruiting qualified workers, from trainers/academics, and from student experiences on secular courses. Some Christians felt that their faith was often disregarded, or even ridiculed, on secular courses (Nash, 2012). This view reflects the experience of one of the authors of this chapter who worked in secular courses between 1981 and 2005. He found that although religious faith was discussed, there was still clear resistance by students to share their faith because of actual or perceived hostility by other students, and some tutors, as some Christian churches were perceived as being sexist, homophobic and undermining professional conditions of service. Students often kept quiet about their faith, rationalising that this was a personal matter despite the likelihood that their faith values would influence their youth work practice. Too often it was at the end of courses that tutors and other students discovered that another student had a religious faith. In this context it is understandable that many Christians would want to study a course that recognised and valued their faith, and included Christian theology in their curriculum, even if some did not want to work within the Christian faith sector. Thus it appears that the Christian Youth Ministry courses that developed from 1998 onwards took a range of Christian students from those who were already working in and committed to the Christian faith sector to those who wanted to work in other voluntary or statutory youth work contexts (Nash, 2012).

It was in the early years of the current century that those with a Muslim faith considered developing JNC qualifying routes, following the development of Muslim Youth Work and the increased numbers of Muslims applying to JNC courses. Young Muslims were in the spotlight post 9/11 and 7/7, and apart from discussions of Islamophobia on secular courses, a distinct Muslim course was developed at Chester College, although this has now closed. Within the emerging Muslim Youth Work sector there were different views on the value of a distinct curriculum for Muslim students on professional qualifying courses.

Safe spaces *and* dialogue on value bases

We believe that professional education courses in youth and community work need to recognise the growing importance of the role of spirituality in youth work, and of faith-based youth work. This is partly because of the size of the Christian sector, and also because of the pressing need to connect more meaningfully with British Muslim youth. Even from a communist atheist position, which is the stance of one of the authors of this chapter, it is important to engage with the social reality of the society and work dialectically with the contradictions therein. Otherwise one develops an arrogance towards the lived realities and material conditions of the people. As Mao Tse-tung stated:

> We are also opposed to 'Left' phrase-mongering. They alienate themselves from the current practice of the majority of the people and from the realities of the day, and show themselves adventurist in their actions.
>
> (Tse-tung, 1937)

The vast majority of the world's population define themselves as religious. In 2002, only 2.5% of the world's population defined themselves as atheists, with a separate 12.7% declaring themselves as non-religious (Encyclopaedia Britannica, 2005). Even in Britain, where only 38% believe in God, a further 40% believe in a 'spirit or life force', with only 20% not believing in a God, a life force or a spirit (2005 Eurostat poll on the religious beliefs of Europeans).

Some see faith traditions as reactionary forces that youth work moved beyond when it became a professional Youth Service post Albemarle, shedding any attempts at proselytising that were evident earlier in the century. Similarly, many see youth work as under threat from present government policies and cutbacks. What can easily get lost in a debate such as this is the overwhelming commonality between faith-based and so-called 'secular' youth work. The professional, political and psychological arguments are well rehearsed. Traditionally these are set on ideological lines – for example, Marx and 'Religion as the Opium of the People' (1843). Marxism's hostility to Christianity was partly based on the historical relationship between capitalism and the church. Marxism is of course post Christian – its criticism of Christianity needs to be examined on the basis of the construct of Christianity that it creates. A common feature of more recent atheistic attacks is the construction of a one-dimensional caricature of religion (e.g. Dawkins' 2006 'The God Delusion').

Often the subtleties are lost, such as the fact that although Marx did see 'religion as the opium of the people' the preceding words read:

> *The wretchedness of religion is at once an expression of, and a protest against, real wretchedness. Religion is the sigh of the oppressed creature, the heart of a heartless world, the soul of soulless conditions.*
>
> (Marx, 1843)

A left wing anti-religious stance also ignores thinkers within the liberation theology movement who have played a central role in revolutionary movements. As with the beginnings of youth work (e.g. the YMCA), still today (through The Children's Society and similar organisations), large numbers of youth workers employed in faith-based settings are practically and passionately engaged with challenging injustice as experienced by working class people around the world.

The notion of praxis (a need for integration of theory and action) is central to both Marxist and faith-based thought. Both seek to transform the world and seek to engage politically to achieve those ends. Both have a sense of an ideal society that provides direction and meaning to our lives. That ideal is achievable through human endeavour. Both agree that we are a long way from that ideal. Notions of salvation and liberation are, at the very least, closely related.

What is most concerning is how the dangers of ideology (and we recognise that religion and politics demand commitment to a set of beliefs) are getting confused with the ability to recognise the spiritual dimension. If defined in an open-ended, not necessarily religious way, spirituality should be seen as central to all youth work practitioners' roles. The decision in 2012 to remove spirituality as a separate National Occupational Standard for youth work was predicated on the assumption that spirituality can be grouped with religion, politics, philosophy and ideology as areas of personal beliefs to explore and choose between. Our view is that developing a sense of spiritual self must precede choices about religion, politics, etc. and as such it is the responsibility of youth workers to promote such development in young people.

In this we agree with Parker J Palmer's view of spirituality as an opening up, an essential part of education, especially in a time when education is increasingly reduced to tests and qualifications:

> *Authentic spirituality wants to open us to truth – whatever truth may be, wherever truth may take us. Such a spirituality does not dictate where we must go, but trusts that any path walked with integrity will take us to a place of knowledge. Such a spirituality encourages us to welcome diversity and conflict, to tolerate ambiguity, and to embrace paradox. By this understanding, the spirituality of education is not about dictating ends. It is about examining and clarifying the inner sources of teaching and learning, ridding us of the toxins that poison our hearts and minds.*
>
> (Parker Palmer, 1993: xi quoted in Smith, 2005)

Therefore we need to recognise the importance of spirituality for all young people, whether they have a religious faith or not, and therefore for all students on JNC courses to understand and promote spirituality in their youth work. The approach at Newman is not pretending to be neutral, it is based on values that question the narrowness of current conceptions of education, as it questions the consumer-driven materialist culture that sees spirituality as irrelevant if not dangerous. Yet we make these choices in an attempt to promote critical analysis and dialogue rather than because we have predetermined ends.

It is also possible that faith-based youth work may be a space to maintain youth work practices and principles, at a time when these are under consider-able threat. The growth of targeted work based on a deficit model of young people, and the undermining of the voluntary relationship, has been more prevalent in the secular sector where funding is dependent on State priori-ties. It is hoped that even those hostile to the growth of faith-based youth work can recognise that there is a commonality in terms of seeing the impor-tance of young people's membership of different groups that help form their identity. Youth work needs defending against those who see membership of cultures, sub-cultures, and even youth groups as getting in the way of 'suc-cessful transitions', and therefore the primary role of the youth worker is to give young people 'reality checks' about successful transitions to adulthood. We stress, along with the In Defence of Youth Work campaign (Taylor, 2009) the importance of association, of autonomous groups, and that young people are not a homogenous group. The defence of youth work would seem to require acceptance of a diverse range of cultural positions. The defence of the Youth Service today will not be helped by retreating into a liberal humanist perspective that alienates those from other perspectives.

We argue that if we really believe that values underpin youth work, and that person centred education (as defined by Brandes and Ginnis, 1986) is the core of youth work then this must be reflected in the professional education of youth workers. Students entering courses already have values from their personal lives and from their youth work experience, albeit this may be little reflected on. Research indicates that there are significant barriers to tutors engaging meaningfully with students around values (Cooper, 2008). Students may start courses more concerned with forming their identity as students, than as youth workers, and may want to ensure that they give the 'right' answers to pass assignments and gain peer approval rather than honestly express their values and principles. However, if it is accepted that personal values should not and cannot be restricted to one's private life then courses must give meaningful space for the critical examination of these values in relation to professional values, principles and ethics, and for the translation of these values into their practice. Our position is that students need to start by reflecting on their personal values by intra dialogue (i.e. within their chosen grouping of Christian, Muslim or non-faith-based practitioners) and then move to inter dialogue with each other. The rationale for this ordering of the curriculum is partly 'to bring things under critical control', to gain clarity and partly to create 'safe spaces' that allow individuals to express themselves openly. As Cooper argues, however, reflection on values cannot be contained within modules, and needs returning to throughout the course. The symbolic meaning of the faith-based pathways to students at Newman is that it opens up the debate that is pursued in a range of modules, and in dialogue that occurs in social settings.

There is a real concern that personal values that derive from political ideologies or religious institutions will result in a separation from and dilution of mainstream youth work (see statement on contested areas in QAA Subject benchmarks in Youth and Community Work, 2009: 9–10). Presumably it is felt that the six named areas (Catholic, Socialist, Islamic, Feminist, Quaker, Jewish) have the potential to promote forms of youth work whose values contradict key principles of the field. Any profession must be mindful of its boundaries and it is possible that in a number of areas contradictions could emerge; for example, participation of young people in decision making, roles of girls and women, position of minority groups, and voluntary relationship in the context of evangelism and conversion. This last area of conversion and the contradiction between indoctrination and youth work principles is one of the most difficult for faith-based youth workers. It is important that students go beyond an over simplistic consumerist view of choice. We agree that intervention, even personal example, by youth workers inevitably means the potential for influence. Youth workers who attempt to leave the space open for young people to make decisions completely by themselves will have that space filled by others. The power of markets and advertising to promote the values of disposable commodities, and valuing ourselves in terms of possessing the latest consumer product is clearly influencing young people, and needs to be challenged by recognising the importance of spiritual values in our materialist culture. The analyses by Freire (1961) and Gramsci (1971) that young people develop 'false consciousness' from capitalism clearly leads to the youth workers being involved in 'conscientisation'. This understanding is usually achieved more easily by students who recognise that they have a set of values (whether from faith or politics) than it is from students whose values are so taken for granted that they are difficult to unearth. It is important that all students can distinguish between broadening and deepening young people's ability to analyse their situation and act accordingly, and indoctrination, which has no place in youth work.

The large numbers of volunteers attracted into youth work by religious or political motivation, and often working in voluntary organisations, means that they will be open to a broader interpretation of youth work than current professional interpretations. These volunteers and part timers make up a significant proportion of those applying for places on JNC qualifying courses. It is inevitable that some will come with over simplistic views about promoting their own values, whether faith-based or not. It could be argued that applicants' values should be tested at interview and those found wanting excluded, but values are often unformed or insufficiently reflected on at this point. The role of JNC courses is to allow the space for meaningful reflection and dialogue, and there is a real danger of applicants and students hiding their views unless this is done in supportive contexts.

This is particularly relevant today, in the context of a backlash against religion and spirituality in the name of atheistic rationality (e.g. from Richard Dawkins, Christopher Hitchens, Martin Amis). However, it is still possible that professional youth work is incompatible with a person's religious or political values, and in this case a judgement will have to be made not to pursue a professional youth work role. It is hoped that the students themselves will realise this early in the course, preferably at interview stage, but if not then tutors have to make these difficult judgements. Our experience so far is that students may struggle but come to find ways to work with the values and principles of youth work whilst recognising that their personal values may differ from some of their colleagues. Just as important as monitoring the boundaries of the profession is establishing dialogue and understanding between the diverse groups within the field of youth work. The role of qualifying courses is to promote understanding and challenge stereotypes that often divide youth workers, just as they do young people.

The Newman way

At Newman, as we will analyse in more detail below, we have since 2007 opted for courses that try to steer a middle path. Our faith-based pathways allow safe spaces for Christian and Muslim students to explore their values and practice but also integrate these students with the main body of students for the majority of their modules, where informed dialogue can take place. The worry about the silencing of faith or it being constructed as a personal issue is also that it does not allow for secular concerns, and sometimes misconceptions, to be discussed. There are tensions, both potential and real, with holding certain faith positions and youth work values, but this tension needs to be held and developed, not silenced and marginalised.

Another argument against creating a distinctive space within JNC courses for students having religious faith is that it will lead to divisions between them and other students (if this is done within the same course, as at Newman) or between JNC qualified workers who will have come through significantly different courses. A common criticism of religious communities (often developed by students in discussions about religion) is that they develop a sense of the other that leads to conflict, often violent, and can also exclude individuals or sub groups that are seen to deviate from accepted norms. This is undoubtedly true but it is a challenge for all, and youth work in particular, to recognise that both diversity and conflict are inevitable and can be positive forces, and this is surely a challenge that should be engaged with on JNC qualifying courses.

It can also be argued that if distinctive spaces are created for Christian and Muslim students (as at Newman) then why not for Jewish, Sikh, Hindu or other faith groups. And why only faith groups? What of gender, race, disability, or sexuality? The view at Newman is that giving precedence to Christians and Muslims can only be justified on the basis of recruitment (based on institutional mission and reputation in terms of Christianity, local demographics in terms of Muslims). More generally, the emphasis on faith as optional pathways, with other cultural categories such as gender or race also being important but being discussed in whole group sessions, is because of the close links between faith and values, and how these are translated into the practice of both Christian and Muslim youth work.

The origins of the faith pathways in the current BA (Hons) Youth and Community Work, and the model followed for integrating faith within a degree open to those with and without religious faith, lies within the Foundation Degrees started in 2007 at Newman College of Higher Education (now Newman University). In 2005 the Catholic field began to consider training opportunities within the sector. Members within the Catholic youth ministry community approached Newman College of Higher Education to investigate the option of a Youth Ministry Foundation Degree which was JNC accredited that had the understanding of Catholic Youth Ministry. Newman was in a position to react to this request as it already fulfilled the minimum NYA requirement that two members of the staff have JNC qualifications, namely the Dean of School, Prof. Stan Tucker and the Chaplain, Margaret Holland.

At the end of 2005, a conference was held to explore what areas of the curriculum would be important for those supporting students on such a course (Training for the Catholic Youth Ministry – Dialogue into Action). Following the event, the first draft of a curriculum was designed to meet the needs of the field. The motivation for developing a JNC qualifying course at Newman was originally to provide a Roman Catholic version of the Christian Youth

Ministry courses developed since 1997 (e.g. CYM, Oasis, Moorlands, Chester).

In parallel to this, Birmingham University had decided on the closure of the Youth Work JNC course situated at Westhill College. The course and college had played an important role in the history of youth work and the training of youth workers in the profession. Long before the emergence of Christian Youth Ministry JNC courses, the Catholic community had many of its workers train at Westhill and gain the JNC qualification there.

In the light of these developments Newman decided to offer a Foundation Degree (FD) in Youth Work. Those involved in the development of the Youth Ministry FD viewed the Youth Work FD as an important opportunity for students to come together from both programmes to share, learn from and challenge one another. The Youth Ministry Curriculum was then adapted to ensure that students could maximise their learning from being together and also allowing the youth ministry students the space to look at the aspects that those who attended the meeting in 2005 felt were essential.

The two FDs were started in 2007, one in Youth Work and the other in Christian Youth Ministry. The model that was validated was to have the first year of the two part time degrees separate, the second year with the two groups working together. With the demise of the Westhill course it was not surprising that the Youth Work FD recruited considerably more students than the Youth Ministry FD (38 to 12) so that when the groups came together in their second year it was a challenge to both groups. Continuity occurred in terms of tutors but the curriculum, and crucially the student group, changed dramatically. Whilst both groups had been prepared for this change by meeting together for one module in their first year, and the tutor groups continued to meet separately in year two, issues still arose in terms of group discussions and dynamics. The extent to which Youth Work and Youth Ministry are distinct areas became an ongoing discussion. The links to the Youth Work National Occupational Standards were important to show the considerable commonalities and, particularly, how spirituality could be an important bridge for both groups. A module specifically on spirituality existed in the FDs as a core module for Youth Ministry students and as an option for Youth Work students. This ran in year two and as many students from the Youth Work degree chose this module as there were Youth Ministry students. This was an indicator of the value and success of promoting dialogue between the two groups, even though the conversations and politics around this module were not easy. One of the decisions that had to be made when we made the move from the FDs to the new

BA was around the module leadership of the faith-based pathways. On the FDs, the Christian Youth Ministry modules were led by Theology tutors, although usually jointly with Youth Work tutors. On the BA, both Christian and Muslim pathway modules are led by Youth Work tutors, but involve Theology tutors. This change reflects the greater integration within the BA, and the aim to ensure that whichever pathway the students choose, they are following parallel curricula that allow all students to come together with similar foundations. This model of steering a middle way between separate and integrated modules for faith based students is also followed for fieldwork practice, where students are expected to undertake at least one, placement in settings that do not reflect their faith position.

Youth work principles and practice, and the link to values and development

Our position is that all JNC courses should critically examine the values that students bring to the course, whether these derive from their personal lives or from their youth work experience (National Youth Agency, 2007: 18). However, we question whether the structure and curricula of JNC courses in HE are moving away from a meaningful engagement with values, preferring to stress the principles of youth work that all students should adopt. If this is so, why? The over-riding concern is that students from all backgrounds may not have the space to express, reflect on and critically examine their values and how these are translated into their youth work practice. A similar argument has been expressed recently within the wider field:

> *A common position is to view youth work as having an ideologically neutral value base and to see a faith value base as being at best additional to this and at worst contrary to youth work values. Given this position it falls upon faith-based workers to defend their value base. However this is a weak position and I contend that all youth workers should consider how their personal values impinge on the work and what is professionally valid.*

> (Green, 2010: 131)

As said, the concern is that if this is not seen as crucial, faith-based workers operating in a hostile climate may repress their views for fear of condemnation by others, or rationalise keeping their views to themselves by seeing their faith as part of their private rather than their professional lives. We argue that it is neither possible nor desirable to keep such a separation of the personal and professional and that both learning and practice is likely to be diminished if this is attempted. If all students are expected to reflect on their personal and professional values, this can legitimise the relevance of faith-based work for both those who hold a faith and those who do not. For the majority of students on JNC courses who do not hold a faith, it is important that they recognise the importance of understanding their own value bases, and critically examining this, as a foundation of youth work practice.

An indication of the practical application of the Newman ethos can be found in the module title of 'personal and professional values' and the follow-up module 'principles and practice of youth and community work'. As tutors we find ourselves in an interesting position, one which enables us to explore with students the 'so called' youth work values of respect, equality of opportunity, person centred approaches and social education. We need to consider that these values are in fact not that unique to youth and community workers. During the academic year, students identify that many professionals hold common values close to their way of working, but the distinctiveness of youth and community work comes from the situations and environments that the work occurs within.

There is a danger of overemphasising the importance of youth work values at the cost of a separatist argument. This misconception misses the fact that many teachers, chaplains, social workers, play workers, community development workers and others may hold the same values. The contemporary discourse generated by the In Defence of Youth Work campaign highlights a range of positions on the principles and practices of youth work. For polemicists such as Tony Taylor, the campaign's founder, 'Youth Work is volatile and voluntary, creative and collective – an association and conversation without guarantees' (Taylor, 2009: 1). By contrast, the research conducted by Davies and Merton (2009) suggests that there might be a divergence between the traditional youth work principles of open access, voluntary relationships and being available for young people and the more recent practice of target setting, targeting young people at risk and accreditation.

The values which we seek to emphasise are those that the student brings with them to the course. We are not talking about the fantasy of 'youth work values'. The students are asked to examine their own value base and the origins, feeders and tensions of these within the first semester of the first year. As previously argued, the importance of creating a space where students can discuss and critically analyse their own and others' values is incredibly important. It provides opportunities to explore areas that students may want to keep hidden, specifically around issues of racism, homophobia and sexism, and to identify the links between religious and other personal values.

For students who have chosen not to take one of the faith pathways within the course, the 'values' module is their opportunity to express what they base their practice on. For some, it is within a solid foundation of humanists' belief in the potential of others, particularly young people. For others it is about simply wanting to put something back into society; a desire to not only change their own lives and futures but those of the young people and communities in which they live and work. Others are from working class and socialist leanings that see the 'profession' of youth and community work as a vehicle for critical, social debate and change.

Some students have not thought about the importance of questioning their own value base or considered its implications before embarking on the course. For these students and many more it is the start of a process of transformative education (Freire, 1961). In addition, there is ever more present a percentage of students that view themselves as not holding any particular stance, faith or political ideology. It is with this group that most of our work is needed. Criticality is central to this position if effective youth work requires 'a constant exercise of choice, recurrent risk-taking, a continuing negotiation of uncertainty' (Davies, 2005: 21).

In our multi-faith and multi-cultural society we rarely get an opportunity to exchange views on what we believe in or not, what values we hold important and whence these values originated. As previously stated it is within this context that we seek to ask students to examine critically their own and others' stance. This questioning is in place to help students develop a dialogical approach which endeavours to enable the different faith, political, and cultural dimensions to be explored and for students to recognize the complexity of their own and others' reality. This sharing of faith, experience and practice also allows for more in-depth discussions as even knowledge is questionable: 'Knowledge relies ultimately on some truths, known without proof or evidence' (Hollis, 1985: 78).

We hold in trust a very special space within the Newman Youth and Community Work course. It is a space which is at one time critical and questioning, sometimes sceptical, whilst at the same time valuing the lived reality of students, especially of those with a Christian or Muslim faith. This space allows, for example, gay Muslim students to discuss the impact of their faith upon them personally and professionally. The practice of questioning Christian, Muslim and generic youth and community practice within critical paradigms is essentially Foucauldian. This critical discourse analysis is encouraged and it is hoped that it ameliorates the practice of hiding behind one's faith, values or ideology.

Conclusion

Dialogue between youth workers from different faiths, and between those with no religious faith, cannot be expected to lead to agreement about values and the path to spiritual development. It can, however, lead to greater understanding of the importance of spiritual development, tolerance towards others, and the boundaries that should exist in youth work in terms of workers imposing their values, religious or otherwise, on young people.

The challenges at Newman University remain considerable with students struggling between the demands of their personal and professional values, and towards gaining an understanding that spiritual development is broader than commitment to a religious faith. The commitment to dialogue enables these debates to be strengthened by involving students and tutors who take different positions.

Our concern is that, at a national level, the paths of faith-based and secular professional training will increasingly divide. The recent decision to remove spirituality as a separate Youth Work National Occupational Standard could be the tipping point that allows this uneasy partnership to crumble. Government policy may well encourage this divide as it is clear that the 'Big Society' proposals do not want to encourage professional youth work, with major cuts to local authority youth services on-going. Even while encouraging initiatives from faith-based and other organisations in the voluntary and third sectors, there is little evidence of the resources needed to sustain them. In our view both secular and faith based youth workers should not be fooled into thinking they have fundamentally different interests for only united can we resist the forces to de-professionalise, and only through dialogue can the faith-based and secular sectors learn from each other. This principle of promoting dialogue among those of the same religious faith as well as between those with different religious faiths and those with no religious faith has relevance for all JNC qualifying courses. We offer the Newman approach as a model that steers a middle way between separation and integration although each JNC qualifying course will have to find a curriculum that reflects both their staff and student make up. We look forward to seeing how others deal with the issues, tensions and contradictions that religious faith presents.

References

Brandes, D. and Ginnis, P. (1986) *A Guide to Student Centred Learning*. Oxford: Blackwell.

Brierley, D. (2003) *Joined Up: An Introduction to Youth Work and Ministry*. London: Pasternoster.

Cooper, S. (2008) Teaching Values in Pre-Qualifying Youth and Community Work Education. *Youth and Policy*, 97/98, 57–72.

Davies. B. (2005) Youth Work A Manifesto of Our Times. reprinted from *Youth and Policy*, 88. Leicester: National Youth Agency.

Davies, B. and Merton, B. (2009) *Squaring the Circle: Findings of a 'Modest' Inquiry Into The State of Youth Work Practice in a Changing Policy Environment*. De Montfort University. http://www.dmu.ac.uk/Images/Squaring%20the%20Circle_tcm6-50166.pdf.

Dawkins, R. (2006) *The God Delusion*. Boston: Houghton Mifflin.

Doyle, M.E. and Smith, M.K. (2002/2013) *Christian Youth Work: A Guide to Reading*. http://www.infed.org/youthwork/b-ywchri.htm.

Encyclopædia Britannica (2005) *Worldwide Adherents of All Religions by Six Continental Areas, Mid-2005*. http://search.eb.com/eb/article-9432620.

Eurostat poll (2005) *Special Eurobarometer 225: Social Values, Science and Technology*. http://ec.europa.eu/public_opinion/archives/ebs/ebs_225_report_en.pdf.

Evans, D. (2012) Personal Communication (based on analysis of NYA Annual Monitoring Survey of JNC Qualifying Courses).

Freire, P. (1961) *Pedagogy of the Oppressed*. Harmondsworth: Penguin.

Gramsci, A. (1971) *Selections from the Prison Notebooks*. London: Lawrence and Wishart.

Green, M. (2010) Youth Workers as Converters. In Banks, S. (Ed.) *Ethical Issues in Youth Work*. London: Routledge.

Hollis, M. (1985) *The Cunning Reason*. Cambridge: Cambridge University Press.

Infed (undated) *Youth Work and Youth Ministry*. http://www.infed.org/christianyouthwork/cyw4.htm.

Infed (undated) *Christian Youth Work and Youth Ministry*. http://www.infed.org/christianyouthwork/index.htm.

Marx, K. (1843) A Contribution to the Critique of Hegel's Philosophy of Right. In O'Malley, J. (Ed.) (1994) *Marx: Early Political Writings*. Cambridge: Cambridge University Press.

Nash, S. (2012) Personal Communication (from Director of Centre Youth Ministry, Nottingham).

National Youth Agency (2007) *Introduction to Professional Validation and Curriculum Requirements, Book 1*. Leicester: NYA.

QAA Subject Benchmarks (2009) *Youth and Community Work*.

Smith, M.K. (2005) *Parker J. Palmer: Community, Knowing and Spirituality in Education*. www.infed.org/thinkers/palmer.htm.

Taylor. T. (2009) *In Defence of Youth Work*. http://in defence of youthwork.wordpress.com/2009/03/11the-open-letter-in-defence-of-youth-work/accessed.

Tse-tung, M. (1937) *On the Relation Between Knowledge and Practice, Between Knowing and Doing*. Speech given in July 1937 at the Anti-Japanese Military and Political College in Yenan, China.

CHAPTER 9

Exploring Interaction Between Young People of Faith: Tools for Understanding?

Phil Henry

This chapter examines an interfaith initiative using some academic 'tools' based broadly within disciplines associated with Symbolic Interactionism. The case study examined here is part of a research project developed through the work of the Multi-Faith Centre at the University of Derby, in creating and supporting The Derby Interfaith Youth Forum (DIYF). In what follows, all the names of participants are pseudonyms as their identity is protected under the ethical agreement for researching with the group.

The complexity of interfaith relations in the UK (Francis et al., 2011) and elsewhere requires an appreciation of 'self-other' interaction and encounter. That is, if the intention is to move to a more sustained relationship-building environment for people with different faith orientations and with those without a professed faith. Examining individual and group identity enables such an approach and, it is argued here, is reinforced by providing additional tools for understanding derived from within the disciplines of sociology and social psychology.

The nature and exploration of identity within the social sciences is variously described, and often contested, as fluid, multi-faceted, hybrid, hyphenated, social and personal to name a few (Ashton et al., 2004; Brubaker and Cooper, 2000; Craib, 1998; Elliott and du Gay, 2009; Hall, 1996; Jenkins, 2008; Woodward, 2002). The usefulness of identity as a concept has indeed been questioned against a background of failing to show cause and effect for actions associated with it (Brubaker, 2004). 'Does identity matter?' asks Jenkins (2008). In keeping with his question, this chapter examines the 'what is' and the 'how' of identity work, set against a background of 'identification'. It explores what we know and how young people of different faiths appreciate their own sense of self against historical discourses embedded in encounter, and how they negotiate meaning making in an interfaith youth forum (Brah, 2007).

Symbolic Interactionism as a discipline focuses on work inspired by Interactionist perspectives on society and, in the context employed here, addresses the meaning of face-to-face encounter as a means to gain a better understanding of 'self-other' relationships. Identification with religious and cultural labels and their meaning for the individual and group (against a background of secularising institutions and influences) are often primary in complex interactions. By examining the interactions within an Interfaith Youth Forum it is possible to see what shapes and sustains conduct within such a group that could benefit youth work practitioners and others in the field.

The UK interfaith context

Interfaith activity in the UK is highlighted in part by what Weller (2005; 2008) refers to as 'Christian, secular and religiously plural'; a three-dimensional socioreligious landscape where private, public and civil society intersect. Interfaith organisations have a relatively short but notable history since 1900, when the International Association for Religious Freedom was formed (previous examples existed but in relative isolation prior to this). Many bi-lateral and tri-lateral groups were established after the First World War and some in direct response to the Holocaust of the Second World War. Organisations included The London Society of Jews and Christians (1927), The World Congress of Faiths (1936), The Council of Christians and Jews (1942). In the last two decades of the twentieth century, and the first decade of the twenty-first, the numbers of organisations seeking to work together for the common good on the basis of shared values has increased dramatically, from around thirty in 1987 to approximately two hundred and forty today (Pearce, 2012). The most significant of these is the national umbrella organisation, The Inter Faith Network for the UK (IFN), established in 1987. The IFN supports the active engagement of faith communities, national, regional and local, as well as having a commitment to education at all levels. It has overseen the public space for the voice of religion and belief groups (including the smaller more marginal organisations) and, as a result, has had a role to play in the creation and shaping of public policy by the last two UK governments. Other organisations including the Three Faiths Forum, St Ethelburga's Centre for

Reconciliation and Peace, Christian-Muslim Forum and Hindu-Christian Forum have all taken positions as dialogic groups to foster better understanding within and across both Abrahamic and Dharmic traditions. Local town and citywide Faiths Forums and Councils have sprung up since the early 1990s and, as a consequence, policy-makers have harnessed the messages of cohesion and engaged such groups in contributing to stronger, safer societies.

These organisational responses to interfaith dialogue and debate still lack a wider community engagement at local level given their often very small numbers of active participants, despite so-called assertions of numerical representation. They do, however, endeavour to sustain grassroots activity, but are sometimes open to accusations, with some notable exceptions, of 'talking' rather than 'doing', particularly when it comes to tangible projects working together in communities. Interfaith youth work, unlike single faith youth work is less well developed. Successive governments in conjunction with IFN UK have sponsored initiatives such as Interfaith Week since 2009, and have encouraged greater youth participation, and a greater general connection to people of no particular faith orientation to extend the reach of Interfaith Week participation. In concentrated efforts, Interfaith Week produces a significant number of youth-related events during that period (Interfaith Network, 2011). There are between 30–50 youth groups actively promoting interfaith youth work in England. However, of those, many are located in schools and colleges or in higher education institutions.

Derby Interfaith Youth Forum (DIYF)

The development of an interfaith youth forum in Derby in 2009/2010 was as a direct result of two intertwined motivating factors. First, the Multi-Faith Centre at the University of Derby had received several requests from young adults to create a loosely defined youth organisation where volunteering opportunities could be created. Second, some of those who sought this course of action supported a successful bid to Volunteering England (VE) with the Multi-Faith Centre, as part of a year long funded pilot project to explore the potential of faith-based volunteering among young people of faith in England between the ages of sixteen and twenty-four. The DIYF only recruits between the ages of 18–24, in keeping with the ethos of a higher education campus, which supports many 'young adults' as a distinct life stage between youth and adulthood (Heath et al., 2009: 4). The organisation is not a Youth Worker led organisation even though it employs a qualified youth worker as its project officer.

It is in the context of the group's development that a separate research initiative developed through the many activities that the Interfaith Forum undertook in that first year (between 2010–2011). Many observations, comments, questions and discussions revealed significant negotiation and construction of 'self-other' relationships in the group. This is of increased interest in light of the lack of literature on the topic of interfaith youth encounter and faith-based volunteering. The research explored a number of aspects, including issues relating to tensions, stigma, stereotyping and representations, and the implications for self-identity and meaning making.

Group demographics

There were 64 active participants in the youth forum in the first year, who self-defined as Muslim (39), Sikh (5), Christian (9), Black Christian (3), Jain (1) and those non-affiliated (7). The demographic make-up of the group and wider research material and findings in relation to the group cannot be included here due to constraints of space.

After the formal project funding came to an end in August 2010 the numbers slowly shrank to between ten and fifteen (by 2012). However, of those that remain committed to the youth forum, all were part of it from its inception and when asked about continued commitment have commented thus:

> The people in the group have become real friends, I feel like I've know them a long time now, and even if we sometimes struggle to get everyone together, we know we have a good relationship and I enjoy seeing everyone.

> (Elana, January 2012)

> I wanted to find out about other faiths but never had a chance till I met the people here; we get on and have worked hard to have more than just a dialogue. Sometimes that has been hard work but I keep coming because others do, we can share a lot even if we only get together once a month now.

> (Kamran, December 2011)

> I'd still come to meetings and eat pizza even if there were only two or three of us turning up; it really makes a difference to meet everyone and share food and thoughts about our worlds especially when we are doing things together.

> (Moussa, October 2011)

The openness and recognition of relationships out of which friendship patterns have been created, and opportunities to meet in surroundings outside those regularly ascribed to individuals from different backgrounds cannot be underestimated. The genuine resolve to see each other, to share food (however basic) and explore with others their experiences is significant to motivate participation.

Symbolic Interactionism: tools for understanding

In order to appreciate how Symbolic Interactionism (SI) might be used to understand conduct in faith-based youth work (and youth work more generally) it is important to briefly examine SI conceptually. It is a sociological theory and was fashioned out of the work of a number of philosophers and social psychologists, but not labelled until the late 1960s. It has its roots in philosophical pragmatism (largely an American conception), associated with John Dewey (1910) and William James (1902), and to a lesser-known extent with George Herbert Mead (1934). Mead published little in his lifetime, but has received recognition posthumously as a direct result of his students collecting his works together and publishing them in *Mind, Self and Society* after his death in 1931. Probably the best-known exponent of his work was Herbert Blumer, who took it upon himself to examine Mead's work. Out of it Blumer coined the term 'Symbolic Interactionism' and identified a general approach to human group life and human conduct (1969: 1). It acknowledges the encounter between human beings, during which signs and symbols of that encounter (physical, verbal and non-verbal) are used to make meaning between us.

SI addresses the subjective meanings imposed in our interpretation of what Erving Goffman (1959: 15) called the 'definition of the situation'. In any given interaction the participants of that encounter will define the situation according to a range of categories, situationally located in the interaction, and in their understanding of the status of the participants and the implication for the symbolic meaning associated with it. Its origins are often seen in the work of Max Weber (1864–1920) who suggested that individuals seek meaning in their interpretation of the world and act according to that interpretation (Bendix, 1946). Symbolic Interactionist theory allows sociologists to examine the micro-sociological detail of encounter. It does however have its critics who assume that such small scale interaction is often in danger of missing the bigger social picture, of 'not seeing the wood for the trees'. Its value in small scale group work, like the youth interfaith forum, is in uncovering what symbolic meaning people develop and rely upon in their interaction with each other.

Understanding something of another's 'definition of the situation' legitimises an individual interaction (if not the individual concerned), and has the potential to create authentic encounter between individuals before any consideration of labels associated with perceptions of others is implied. The confidence developed through interaction enhances the skills of those in the group to recognise intentionally conveyed misinformation by either feigning or deceit. It also helps them to assess the promissory character of personal face-to-face encounter, which may later, when the individual is not in their presence, allow inferences which make a meaningful attempt to measure the true value of that encounter (Goffman, 1959: 14). Many judgements and decisions associated with experience come through inference. Although implicitly and inherently applied by most people, few of us analyse how important inference is to our ability to decide what is appropriate in encounters and its effect on intention. Volition informs, and is informed by, action(s) in encounter and interaction. The cognitive process affecting our consciousness completes a cycle of 'action-intention-action'.

DIYF members created spaces with the support of workers where it became an acceptable part of their interaction to ask the difficult questions about a range of topics, without fear of offending or of being perceived as voyeuristic in their intention. This correlates directly with learning how to read and respond to the symbolism associated with words and gesture. This includes understandings about aspects of faith and how they affect thinking about topics such as: gender segregation, euthanasia, abortion, sexual health, the environment, women in religion or violent extremism (to name only a few). It also reflects more mundane enquiries by group members about why certain forms of dress are associated with some religions and not others, why there is controversy in the public discourse about the wearing of open and full face veils (hijab and niqab), or why the Mormon (Latter Day Saints) religious experience is dogged with questions about polygamous marriages?

The religious and cultural influences on individuals' lives can be associated with their familial background, cultural affirmation or denial of their heritage, or a continual shift between broad categories of understanding about the self. For example, we might shift between understandings of the self as an objective 'me' or a subjective 'I' and where the self fits into the multiplicity of identities we connect with and are connected with through our life course and worldview. This is often described by Interactionists as 'identity work'.

There are three key aspects to take account of in understanding interactions, these are adopted by Blumer from Mead and explained thus:

> *(1) That human beings act towards things on the basis of the meanings that things have for them; (2) that the meanings of such things is derived from, or arises out of, the social interaction that one has with one's fellows, and (3) that these meanings are handled in and modified through, an interpretative process used by the person in dealing with the things he encounters.*
>
> (Blumer, 1969: 2)

The question of acting towards objects which have meanings associated with them allows the actor to derive meaning according to the situation in which the encounter takes place; 'defining the situation'. There was an encounter, for example, where a male in the group appeared to want to 'define the situation' by presenting his version of what he might see as the prevailing view, apparently assuming his 'definition of the situation' had the moral authority over the views he claims are held by others. He asserted that females had less of a role to play in religious life than males. The meaning and the interpretative framework used in such an encounter are fundamental when shaping responses, actions and attitudes among groups and individuals. The female in that particular interaction responds by challenging the prevailing view and that of her male colleague, both in the verbal and non-verbal responses she provides. At the point of interaction is the space in which we learn how she reads and recognises what her male associate both 'gives' and 'gives off' (Goffman, 1959: 14) in the cues (verbal and non-verbal) he presents and in the message he is expressing. The skill of the female participant in this encounter is to formulate a response which depends on her assessing the initial information one first acquires in the interaction. This initial information commits the male participant to the type of projection he is offering without pretence, and as the interaction progresses the female can, through reading the initial line of enquiry, modify or add in information in making a case for a contrary view. In order to avoid the 'definition of the situation' becoming too disrupted or even breaking down (which could then create a more embedded potential conflict) there may be a necessity for subtle positioning which requires the use of the moral character or imperative associated with the interaction. In other words if, as Goffman (1959) suggests, an individual is projecting a 'definition of the situation' in which the moral character is invoked, they would have an expectation that others would value and treat them in an appropriate way.

Recognition of both the projection of the other and a concern for the other's position (even if it is not an agreeable one) will promote deep listening through which a level of equilibrium is maintained in the interaction as it authenticates the process, without necessarily agreeing with its content. When the question of exerting a moral position is employed in interaction one also implicitly forgoes all claims to be things he/she does not appear to be, if one is to be treated as genuine in the encounter.

Even a simple handshake as a greeting is symbolic of many other responses. If you are Muslim and female you may feel constrained by modesty in your own religious practice not to shake hands, particularly with males, and non-Muslims. The provenance of the decision not to do so is arguable, but the reality of the situation we found within the group was a common assumption neither clearly religiously or culturally ascribed, that in the name of modesty shaking the hands of males was not an appropriate act. If then the 'definition of the situation' is disrupted by an uncomfortable encounter that might otherwise assume a greeting, how does the worker facilitate that? Our experience was to examine barriers and opportunities to normative interaction by addressing the potential religious and cultural dynamics known among the participants in the group and to reflect upon their personal positions in relation to contact. This included hand shakes, touching others as a friendly gesture by, for example, patting of the hand or shoulder or back, or holding an arm as part of a gesture. The symbolic meaning of which, in general, denotes friendship and comradeship, and yet in terms of interpretative processes in the group, could also symbolically represent unwanted attention or immodest action.

We explored where disruption of the definition of the situation occurred by examining what was verbalised as well as the non-verbal actions associated with it in role play and scenario building exercises. Through this, the protective practices group members put in place in their interactions were examined and the implications for why this was the adopted strategy unpacked. What we found was the implicit desire of most people to 'manage impressions' being created in the interaction by employing tact. The rationale for this is generally to save the mutually formed agreement of the 'definition of the situation' to allow the smooth passage of the interaction and to safeguard any misplaced impression that might otherwise be received by any one or all the participants in any given interaction. This tactic is what Goffman (1959: 25) refers to as seeing modesty in one's claims and reasonableness in their projected expectations. Such practices, more often than not, work in an individual's favour to sustain positive interaction.

Making sense of conceptions of the 'self' and identification

In order to make sense of why people do what they do, we need to take account of the aspects of identification alluded to in Mead's (1934) conception of the 'self' as designated in common use of the words 'I' and 'me'. He describes the relationship as follows:

> The 'I' is the response of the organism to the attitudes of the others; the 'me' is the organized set of attitudes of others which one himself assumes. The attitudes of the others constitute the organized 'me', and then one reacts toward that as an 'I'.
>
> (Mead, 1934: 174)

The 'to and fro' of this process allows internal interrogation as an 'I' and also the ability to see oneself as an 'object' that one perceives to have control over; a 'me'. The perception of others towards an individual self is reflected by our self-understanding, which recognises the social self only because of a realisation of how others in society have an influence over that individual self.

The subject of social interaction and how one sees oneself is affirmed not only by Goffman (1959; 1968; 1970; 1972) but also in the work of Charles Cooley (1922). Goffman uses a range of texts that deal with interaction using a 'dramaturgical metaphor', 'social order', and 'interaction ritual' to name but a few. Cooley, like Mead, sees the essence of the self as cognitive; 'in other words a self is formed through knowledge acquired by mediated experience' (Best, 2003: 114). Mead acknowledges that the internalization of the attitudes of others is represented by the notion of the 'generalised other', and by contrast those with whom one is primarily socialized he refers to as 'significant others', which extends to partners, spouses and other close family members or friends. Cooley (1922) saw the interaction of people mediated as a 'looking glass', in what is called his 'Looking Glass Self'. He suggests there are three steps in the conception of his theory:

> (1) That as human beings we look at our appearance from the perspective of the other, (2) we attempt to imagine the judgment of the other about us, and (3) we use the above information to develop feelings about our self, such as self-respect or embarrassment.
>
> (Best, 2003: 114)

We are seen, Cooley conceives, and understand ourselves, as if we are looking in a mirror; the reflection is in the eyes of the person with whom we are in interaction. How we believe others perceive us shapes how we see ourselves, as if through their eyes. This is borne out by participant responses and is a significant factor when attempting to respond to the way individuals react within a group. An example of which is reflected in Zahid's comments below:

> It was quite important because I seen it [joining the youth forum] as an opportunity . . . a lot of people do not really know about the religion [Islam]. They will see a man with a beard and traditional clothes and they feel like whoa . . . 'I'm a bit wary of this person' you know because the media is propagating this image that all Muslims wear beards, they are extreme, they are fundamentalists, which we are not.
>
> (Zahid, 2010).

The quotation above exemplifies how one believes one's religious group to be perceived, and the consequence of how you understand yourself in relation to that perceived or imagined reality. We look at our appearance from the perspective of the other, attempt to imagine the judgment of the other about us, and use that information to develop feelings about our self, such as self-respect or embarrassment – both of which are reflected in the comments about media driven Muslim perceptions. In scenarios explored by the youth group, participants saw how they recognised the reaction of others but, more importantly, how their recognition was based on what they perceived the other to be thinking of them. The mirror image was a powerful tool around which definitions of the situation could be assessed.

Goffman (1959) uses a similar analogy where he explores the front stage actions of individuals and groups, explained as being in a public space, and the back stage actions in a more private space. In the latter there is less chance of losing face through embarrassment, or being stereotyped or stigmatized – another area where he researched the social world, in his work on asylums (1968). The social norms and consensual or constraining factors of any particular situation are managed to present the actor in the best possible light. This approach seeks to manage the interface between the 'self-image' and the 'public-image' (Wetherell, 2010).

Conclusion

It is not enough simply to assert an identity (in a youth group or elsewhere), it must be validated, or not, by those with whom we have contact. While we can all control, to a degree, the signals we send out about ourselves, we are ultimately at a disadvantage as we cannot guarantee their correct reception or interpretation. For Goffman (1970) this is described as the 'interaction order'. Such an 'order', when understood by members of the DIYF, built confidence in individual and social selves which assisted with the smooth running of their many interactions. Goffman's own sense of selfhood is not undermined by what critics refer to as his failing to examine the authentic self beneath the performance. Rather, he adopts a response to the sense of 'a self' that he suggests is both active and strategic, relying on the levels of belief an individual puts into his/her own sense of reality to locate an authentic self beneath the performance which he suggest is the 'strategic self in action'.

> His [Goffman's] goal in analysing these many forms of interaction was to study the ground rules, which people follow when carrying through their lines of action in situations which they share with others.
>
> (Cheal, 2005: 149)

This is precisely what the youth group had undertaken in their own efforts to establish their form of social order. It is important to note here that commonality has a part to play in the reconciliation of the 'ritual' that is 'everyday' social interaction. Social order is predicated on the veneration of commonality in interaction and it is that which, when reproduced, maintains order. When it comes to saving faces or 'managing impressions' people also co-operate to save each other's. As Goffman (1972) identified quite rightly, the majority of interaction is orderly with minimum conflict. This is generally true of the DIYF, outside of a few individual instances of one-on-one tension. The ground rules facilitate this pursuit of personal social situations with most people arriving at a working consensus on the 'definition of the situation'. Goffman concludes, however, that there is always the tendency that people do not always reach agreement based on the real feelings they hold, but will rather suppress their real feelings and beliefs and only express those others are likely to agree with. What is apparent with the DIYF was that the greater the connection and confidence of self-conception with others in the group (built up over time and with familiarity), the less likely they were to suppress their real feelings. Individuals did speak out where they felt it important to do so.

It is apparent that to understand how young people from diverse faith-based backgrounds understand themselves and others in a group is essential. They come to a group like the DIYF with a range of self-oriented and other-oriented labels. Making sense of themselves as agents depends on recognition and/or rejection, acceptance or indifference to the 'groupings' they are associated and associate with. That can be constraining, for example, in relation to intergenerational tension because it is sometimes difficult to have conversations within familial groups about, for example, gendered or sexual identities. On the other hand, in-group experiences of a youth forum can facilitate (peer-to-peer and with workers) appropriate levels of debate. Similarly, the setting, ethos, ground rules, training opportunities and facilities made available in the context of the group, and the relationship building that flows from interaction, individually and in group settings, are empowering. They have developed conduct conducive to self-other understanding, respect and in-group affirmation leading to greater self-worth and self-esteem. This is as a direct consequence of awareness on the part of the workers and the participants of the opportunities and barriers presented by grounding interactions in mutually respecting personal encounter and exploring how that occurs. The learning from that experience removes the potential to 'other' and creates a personal space in which each has an authentic position, regardless of the issue and how banal or emotive it might be.

References

Ashton, R.D., Deaux, K. and McLaughlin-Volpe, T. (2004) An Organizing Framework for Collective Identity: Articulation Significance of Multi-dimensionality. *Psychological Bulletin*, 130: 80–114.

Bendix, R. (1946) Max Weber's Interpretation of Conduct and History. *American Journal of Sociology*, 51: 6, 518–26.

Best, S. (2003) *Social Theory*. London: Sage Publications.

Blumer, H. (1969) *Symbolic Interactionism: Perspectives and Methods*,. New Jersey: Prentice Hall.

Brah, A. (2007) Non-binarized Identities of Similarity and Difference. In Wetherell, M., Leflèche, M. and Berkeley, R. *Identity, Ethnic Diversity and Community Cohesion*. London: Sage Publications.

Brubaker, R. and Cooper, F. (2000) Beyond "Identity". *Theory and Society*, 29: 1–47.

Brubaker, R. (2004) *Ethnicity Without Groups*. Cambridge, MA: Harvard University Press.

Cheal, D. (2005) *Dimensions of Sociological Theory*. Basingstoke: Palgrave Macmillan.

Cooley, C.H. (1922) *Human Nature and the Social Order*. Chicago: University of Chicago Press.

Craib, I. (1998) *Experiencing Identity*. London: Sage Publications.

Dewey, J. (1910) *How We Think*. Lexington, MA: DC Heath.

Elliott, A. and du Gay, P. (2009) Editor's Introduction. In *Identity in Question*. London: Sage Publications.

Francis, L.J., Williams, E. and Village, A. (2011) Research Note: Multi-Faith Britain and Family Life: Changing Patterns of Marriage, Cohabitation, and Divorce Among Different Faith Groups 1983–2005. *Journal of Contemporary Religion*, 26: 1, 33–42.

Goffman, E. (1959) *The Presentation of Self in Everyday Life*. Harmondsworth: Penguin.

Goffman, E. (1968) *Asylums: Essays on the Social Situation of Mental Patients and Other Inmates*. Harmondsworth: Penguin.

Goffman, E. (1970) *Strategic Interaction*. Blackwell: Oxford.

Goffman, E. (1972) *Interaction Ritual: Essays on Face-to-face Behaviour*. Harmondsworth: Penguin.

Hall, S. (1996) Introduction: Who Needs Identity? In Hall, S. and du Gay, P. (Eds.) *Questions of Cultural Identity.* London: Sage Publications.

Heath, S., Brooks, R., Cleaver, E. and Ireland, E. (2009) *Researching Young People's Lives.* London: Sage Publications.

Interfaith Network UK (2011) *Young People and Inter Faith Encounter.* [http://www.interfaith.org.uk/publications/youthresourcelow-res.pdf.

James, W. (1902) *The Varieties of Religious Experience: A Study in Human Nature.* London: Longman Green.

Jenkins, R. (2008) *Social Identity.* (3rd edn.) London: Routledge.

Mead, G.H. (1934) *Mind, Self and Society.* (Ed. Morris, C.W.) Chicago: University of Chicago Press.

Pearce, B. (2012) The Inter Faith Network and the Development of Interfaith Relations in Britain. In Woodhead, L. and Catto, R. (Eds.) *Religion and Change in Modern Britain.* London: Routledge.

Weller, P. (2005) *Time for a Change: Reconfiguring Religion, State and Society.* London: T. & T. Clark.

Weller, P. (2008) *Religious Diversity in the UK: Contours and Issues.* London: Continuum.

Wetherell, M. (2010) The Field of Identity Studies. In Wetherell, M. and Mohanty, C.T. (Eds.) *The Sage Handbook of Identities.* London: Sage Publications.

Woodward, K. (2002) *Understanding Identity.* London: Arnold.

CHAPTER 10

The Place of Doubt in Youth Work – A Personal Journey

Bernard Davies

Engaging with faith; rediscovering doubt

How are youth workers in Muslim communities dealing with the increasing pressures which face those communities, and above all their young people, simply because they are Muslim? This was the concern – as real today, it seems to me, as it was eight years ago – which prompted me to go to the first Muslim youth work conference in Birmingham in December 2005 and which, much to my surprise, led three months later to my making a brief input into the second conference. Even more unexpectedly, this was followed by three years as a trustee of the organisation which emerged from those conferences, the Muslim Youth Work Foundation (MYWF) and by the *Youth and Policy* article, on 'doubt in youth work', on which this chapter is based (Davies, 2006). This all happened in the aftermath of the July 2005 London bombings. This period, in which the 'war on terror' rhetoric was being ramped up across the world, had increasingly damaging consequences for Muslim communities in Britain and, in particular, for how Muslim young people were seen and treated. Overall, the political climate in which Muslim youth workers were practising was, it seemed to me, one of moral panic that ensured a relentless, and overwhelmingly hostile, image-shaping by both the UK government and the media. As a result, this segment of our youth population was in effect being told to make a crude and unjust identity choice: your religion or your nation. (For a full updated and critical discussion of these developments and the pressures they produced see Khan, 2013, especially Chapter 8).

As a Jew who, as I explain more fully later, had rejected Zionism in his teens and become increasingly appalled by Israel's brutally oppressive policies, this demand made of Muslim young people now strikes me as especially ironic.

For years I have watched the Jewish community in Britain – without ever attracting government or media criticism or even attention – actively encouraging its young people to look to Israel as their potential 'home' and providing them with opportunities and indeed resources for transferring their national loyalty to it. Indeed, this ultimately – and undisguisedly – was, and remains, the raison d'être of a number of high profile and indeed highly regarded Jewish youth organisations.

At the time of my initial contacts with my new Muslim colleagues, my immediate challenge was how to locate some of our conversations in the context of my definition of myself as secular – as a sceptic who was and still is untouched by, and uncomprehending of, notions of the divine and transcendental. These discussions, I found, were requiring me to look again, more critically, at these standpoints and in particular at my image of 'faith' and indeed faiths. Some such rethinking seemed unavoidable, for example, when Muhammad Khan, who was instrumental in setting up MYWF, introduced me to the early thirteenth century Sufi poet, Rumi, and his thought that:

The way leads through doubt to the shore of truth
Just as an answer is reached through questioning

With the paradoxes embedded in these verses immediately striking chords with how I struggled to understand the world, I was prompted to retrace some of the stages of my past 'identity journey'. This certainly did not lead me to reject the sceptic label: in fact, if anything, it resulted in my embracing it more confidently. It did, however, bring to the surface searching questions about its origins, the perspectives on which it rested and some of the contradictions within it. More specifically, it encouraged me to re-examine the very personal experiences of family, community and culture which had contributed to it and, rather than treating such influences and their impacts as givens, to become clearer and more explicit about them.

When the personal meets the professional

For this preoccupation with the personal in an essay on youth work practice, I make no apology. Though it certainly needs to be checked and balanced by disciplined reflection, ultimately all 'practice-with-people' is substantially delivered by and through the subjectivity of the human being. This is as it should be since this subjectivity is arguably the carrier of the passion, the compassion and the empathy on which all good practice rides.

All this, for me, is especially true for youth work since at its heart is a

130 YOUTH WORK AND FAITH

commitment to developmental and person-centred approaches which only resonate with young people when they feel they are meeting the person as well as the worker. This means, at least in youth work, that the personal and the professional can never be wholly separated – that seeking to remove ourselves, our values, our perceptions and our interpretations from our work is never a realistic option. It also helps explain why a key defining feature of the practice is the acceptance and even encouragement of a relatively porous boundary between the personal and the professional. (See, for example, *In Defence of Youth Work*, 2011: 45).

This is why, in order to explain the place of doubt in such a practice, it seemed appropriate – indeed necessary – to start by tracing my personal journey, especially of ideas and values. As so often happens, negotiating this process turned out to be a stage in its own right in that journey as I discovered new connections between, and new meanings in, past experiences which for years had remained under- or even un-interpreted.

What Jewish identity?

For the focus of this piece, I need to start with my Jewish background and what I regard as the positive ways in which it helped shape my early years. The religious content of these influences took the form of a selective range of practices and rituals largely associated with birth, confirmation (barmitzvah), marriage and death and with the observance of the Jewish High Festivals and the Passover. Stopping well short of what any strictly orthodox Jew would have expected, these seem in hindsight to have acted more as the glue of family and community bonds than as an expression of reverence for God and the sacred or even of spirituality. Moreover, looking back, I realise that their very routine, and the boredom this induced, overrode all other responses and left me untouched, both intellectually and emotionally.

For most days of the year, in fact, including most Saturdays (the Sabbath), life was predominantly secular – British secular. The main foci were not that different from those of my non-Jewish friends, though many of them did have some distinctively Jewish attributes and nuances. There was – of course – family, which for me, unthinkingly, was 'extended', requiring the negotiation of some hugely complex and sometimes conflicting inter-relationships with and amongst eleven aunts and uncles and their spouses and eighteen cousins, many of whom I would see at least once a week. There was my father's job in one of those traditional Jewish trades, garment-making, which in his case meant years spent in a factory making waterproof coats – and breathing in toxic fumes which might well have contributed to his early death. There was my own and my brother's education – valued amongst Jews for its own sake as well as for the access it promised to opportunities my parents had never had. My own route through education was eased by my being one of the first beneficiaries of the 1944 Education Act. And there was recreation – especially agonising over whether (as even then they did only occasionally) Manchester City would finish above Manchester United!

Then there were politics and the political activism which came with them. For my personal journey, these – unashamedly socialist and deeply committed to social and economic justice – were crucial. Integral to the Jewish culture and identity in which I grew up, the roots of these values, I realised many years later, lay in distant and now lost Eastern Europe communities. For it was from these that, in the last decades of the nineteenth century, thousands of Jews, including some of my family, had been driven by organised, violent anti-Semitic attacks – the pogroms. Many of these Jews, brought up on the questioning forms of debate which were deeply embedded in Jewish religious education and culture, had already been involved in the radical (and indeed sometimes revolutionary) movements confronting the autocratic and oppressive regimes of their countries of origin.

These emigrants thus did not start from assumptions of compliance with or even respect for the status quo, whether institutional or intellectual. On the contrary, deeply entrenched within their Jewishness was a strong tradition of divergent and *doubting* ways of thinking which at that time, *within* the tradition, extended to passionate debates over the then still emergent notion of Zionism. Significantly, at the heart of their anti-Zionist challenge was often the question: 'Why use our energies seeking a separate Jewish homeland when the real struggle for the Jews is for justice and equality here, in the countries where we live?'

Looking back over two-plus generations, I now like to see myself as a product of that culture and tradition – though not, ironically, of that original critique of Zionism. In that period (the later 1940s and 1950s) and in the north Manchester community where I grew up, few had experienced the Holocaust directly. Indeed its meaning only became personal for me many years later when a survivor married into our family. Nonetheless, its images and impacts were still so recent and vivid for that post-1945 generation that all the then significant figures in my life simply took it for granted that a Jewish homeland was needed. As a result, as I began to face just how radically the Zionist project conflicted with my wider commitments to justice and the then still emerging notion of human rights. I found myself, in my later teens and early twenties, dealing with one of my earliest and more painful struggles with the discomforts of doubt – with, significantly, my main support in setting off on this crucial stretch of my journey coming from a youth worker.

Beyond the Zionist challenge, however, and for me confusingly contradictorily even after all these years, vague but still credible recollections remain from my later childhood of wider 'left' political conversations swirling around me, often suffused with powerful feelings of anger about inequality and injustice. In these, my father features most prominently, captured still in a recalled sense of his euphoria on the day of the 1945 Labour victory for which he had worked. They include, too, memories of a close family friend sitting in our kitchen a decade or so on still refighting the battles of the International Brigade and the Spanish Civil War.

From self-reflection to doubt

Though my father died when I was 17, through these and other much more targeted conversations, he introduced me to the idea of self-reflective thinking long before I had ever heard the term or it had become part of my professional jargon. Insisting on the primacy of intellectual honesty, with myself as well as with others, he left me with rules of engagement such as:

- Start from the proposition that our understanding of world is incomplete – a staging post along the way to (perhaps) some greater clarity.
- Never assume the conclusion you've reached today is the final one.
- Face the possibility – indeed the likelihood – that today's certainties will look jaded and even indefensible next year or in five years time.
- Always entertain the possibility that the next question will turn out to be much more interesting or challenging or revealing than the last answer.

However, underlying all this was a deeper, if often implicit, message: that doubt is not to be treated as an aberration. Doubt is not an unfortunate obstacle in the way of achieving the comfortable life, to be eliminated as quickly and as painlessly as possible. For me, it stands therefore in sharp contrast to how Margaret Thatcher presented it when quoting St Francis of Assisi on the day she became Prime Minister. She, in effect, equated it with discord, error and despair and hoped that 'where there is doubt, may we bring faith'. Honestly engaging with doubt may at times even mean acting *in* faith. However, what in my view remains inescapable is that doubt is a defining feature of the human condition, to be valued and embraced as a protection against dogma and, more positively, as a vital prompt to pushing beyond certainty into the unknown and the unresolved. It is the fuel that drives personal growth and societal renewal.

So, in this context, what do I mean by doubt? The Oxford dictionary talks about 'the act or process of questioning truth or fact. That which is open to question'. Roget's Thesaurus equates 'to doubt' with 'to demur', 'to puzzle' and 'to hesitate'. I have also now come across a throw away definition of science which, somewhat counter-intuitively, described it as 'organised doubt' within which 'falsity [is] its only certainty' (Vernon, 2011). The focus here, it is important to note, are not on doubts (in the plural) – about specific ideas or actions or choices. It is about doubt as a generic concept – a lens through which to refract what goes on in the world in order to assess how to act in and, as importantly, *on* that world rather than just receive whatever it throws up.

Asserting a continuously questioning approach of this kind should not of course be taken as a rejection of adherence to some core values. Under this rubric I would list a belief in individuals' capacity to go where they may never have dreamed of going, collectively as well as separately. This includes their right to the freedom, the opportunity and the means to do this and, as they proceed, a right to be treated equally and justly – with respect, care and compassion.

However, by definition, these are not statements of *knowing* – based on *proof* of their absolute validity or of their universal applicability. They are what they say they are: statements of belief, of conviction, requiring us to proceed on the 'as if' principle – as if they were 'true'. Indeed, what 'real life' confirms repeatedly is that because such 'truths' can conflict with each other, we have at times to face choosing *between* them and thereby weakening any claim to their absoluteness. What we are required to do, then, is pick our way through different – even competing – 'goods'. At the inter-personal level, for example, this may mean breaking a confidentiality agreement with a young person in order to protect them from harm or even death. In a much more public sphere – as the Leveson Inquiry has shown only too starkly – it may mean limiting freedom of the press in order to respect personal privacy.

For, in the end, the process of applying our values and beliefs, including ones that are most deeply felt, requires *judgement*. And this in turn assumes questioning, self-questioning, the avoidance of the arrogance of certainty – an exploration of alternative interpretations and possibilities. In these processes doubt acts as a crucial safety valve.

So . . . what has any of this to do with youth work?

In taking on this question, I need to start by acknowledging the contribution to my thinking of Bryan Merton with whom I was working during 2006 on a training module entitled 'Ambiguity, identity and conflict'. Included as an appendix to the original *Youth and Policy* article, on which this chapter is based, this was a grounded example of how the values and aspirations for which I was arguing might, in a very modest way, be explored through practice with young people (Davies, 2006: 76–9).* Underpinning the module was the hope that youth workers might be encouraged to become more proactive in supporting young people to engage with doubt and with the subsequent ambiguous and conflicting choices around values and actions. Underpinning it, too, was the assumption that such support was likely to be particularly important to young people as they confronted questions central to defining a confident personal identity – such as:

Who am I now?
What is distinctive and special about me?
Who do I hope and want to become?
What do I believe?
Where do I belong?

These questions are integral to young people moving away from the 'taken-for-granted' certainties of childhood and into the more conscious and less clear-cut self-expectations that emerge as they begin to deal with the world around them in more independent terms. One of the features – indeed strengths – of this transition is that it gives them the time and space to test out alternative versions of themselves including different, even experimental, answers to those key identity questions.

This process has never been straightforward or tension-free in Western industrialised societies. The choices they face, some personally testing and highly contradictory, can leave young people searching and unsure. In the past, however, some guidelines have been on offer, implicitly or explicitly, in the form of expectations arising from a young person's family, class, gender, community, religion and ethnicity. These of course have often set highly constraining boundaries to their personal aspirations and development, limiting their realisation of that individual potential and achievement discussed earlier.

---

* The article that includes the training module resource is in Youth and Policy No. 92 and this can be accessed online via www.youthandpolicy.org.

They have also, however – and this is where the contradictions can be felt more keenly and personally – provided supports in that negotiation of difficult value choices and in that wider process of self-definition.

For young people today, where these markers have not already crumbled, they are being put under huge strain by fast and unrelenting economic, social and technological change. A multiplicity of possible responses to a widening range of choices is being communicated from all around the world. Individuals may then be left to make more and more of them on their own, based largely on their personal judgements of meanings and consequences. All this can leave people, and not just young people, uncertain, overwhelmed – and reaching for solutions which not only eliminate doubt but treat it as unacceptable. For example, in a review of a book on 'expert forecasting', Dylan Evans notes a widespread aversion to uncertainty even amongst such 'experts' as the international intelligence community. This leads to a tendency to suppress doubt because it does not fit with policy preconceptions and requirements more generally (Evans, 2011). In response to pressures exerted by politicians, the media and anxious parents and communities, we are all open to resolving complex questions and dilemmas by settling for simplistic one-dimensional answers. At best this might mean reaching for the less painful solutions and the less taxing ways of reaching them – to conclude, for example, 'If you are not with us, you are against us' and to operate on the one-dimensional principles of 'either/or'; 'us or them'; 'I'm in – so you're out'; 'if-it's-not-this-then it-must-be-that,' and (often literally) 'black, or white.' At worst, Evans suggests, when the need for closure becomes paramount, 'any answer, even a wrong one, is preferable to remaining in a state of confusion and ambiguity' (2011: web). All this, he concludes, points to the need for training in a special kind of 'risk-intelligence' – perhaps not too dissimilar to that for which Bryan Merton and I were searching and perhaps as important as, the now widely fashionable, emotional intelligence.

This then sets the wider context in which young people have to negotiate those conflicts of values, loyalties and identities, where the demands are often ambiguous and open to a range of interpretations. These can become, or can come to seem, intractable leaving young people with ambivalent feelings about the effects of the choices they have to make on themselves and on others about whom they care deeply.

For young people, however, there are particular reasons for addressing these issues very directly. As was suggested earlier, they are after all at a stage in their lives when they are still experimenting with who they are and who they want to be. If then they do not see dilemmas and choices and *un-certainties* as inescapable features of everyday living; if they do not begin to *embrace* difference rather than treat it as a threat; if they do not recognise the *excitement* of doubt; and if they do not develop the confidence to face these experiences and learn to deal with these tough choices in less stereotyped ways, then they are unlikely to do so later.

And what more appropriate an environment for doing this than that provided by youth work? This after all is a practice which is itself rooted in uncertainty and risk-taking. It is practice that operates without the supportive structures of the teacher's national curriculum, the social worker's common assessment framework or the career adviser's listings of course opportunities and career pathways. By definition, it is a practice which works with the intrinsic unpredictability of young people *choosing* to come (but not necessarily to stay). It is a practice which focuses not on where 'young people in general' are starting from but on where *these* young people are starting – the ones who have actually engaged. It starts from *their* interests and concerns, on what *they* are signalling they want and need from *this* youth work encounter, on *their* uncertainties and doubts. It is a practice which gives as much weight to the fluidity and changeability of their *here-and-now* as to their future. Building from these emergent prompts, it is practice which is then committed to developing educational programmes whose outcomes cannot be specifically predicted in advance. It is hardly surprising therefore that even Her Majesty's Inspectorate – albeit many years ago! – pointed out that, while youth workers remain 'fully aware of the complexities of what they do' and are 'well rehearsed in the basics', much of their practice happens 'on the wing' (HM Inspectorate, 1987: 2, 20).

Here, for me, is the point where my personal struggle to work actively and openly with doubt meets my understandings of what is needed today for work with young people, in faith-based no less than in secular settings. My bottom line (my judgement!) is that if, as youth workers, it is certainties we are seeking to pass on to young people then, whatever their background or identity, we will be doing them a great and long-term disservice. Youth workers least of all, I conclude, can afford to be, or to work, without doubt.

I end with a poem which I found on the wall of a young people's centre. It is written, I later discovered, by Christina Henry (2006) and it had been posted there by a young person who at the time was in custody – and who, it would seem, was well versed in living with doubt.

Risk Taking Is Free . . .
To laugh is to risk appearing the fool
To weep is to risk appearing sentimental
To reach out for another is to risk involvement
To expose feeling is to risk exposing your true self
To place your ideas, your dreams before the crowd is to risk their loss
To love is to risk not being loved in return
To live is to risk dying
To hope is to risk despair
To try is to risk failure
But risk must be taken, because the greatest hazard in life is to risk
* nothing*
The person who risks nothing, does nothing, has nothing, and is
* nothing.*
He may avoid suffering and sorrow, but he simply cannot learn, feel,
* change, grow, love, live.*
Chaired by his certitudes, he is a slave, he has forfeited freedom
Only a person who risks . . . Is free.

References

Davies, B. (2006) The Place of Doubt in Youth Work: A Personal Journey. *Youth and Policy*, 92, 69–79.

Evans, D. (2011) Future Babble by Dan Gardner – Review. *The Guardian*, 7 May. http://www.guardian.co.uk/books/2011/may/07/future-babble-dan-gardner-review.

Henry, C. (2006) Risk-taking is Free. http://www.poemhunter.com/poem/risk-taking-is-free/.

HM Inspectorate (1987) *Education Observed 6: Effective Youth Work*. London: Department of Education and Science.

In Defence of Youth Work (2011) *This is Youth Work: Stories from Practice*. http://www.indefenceofyouthwork.org.uk/wordpress/?page_id=837.

Khan, M.G. (2013) *Young Muslims, Pedagogy and Islam: Contexts and Concepts*. Bristol: Policy Press.

Vernon, M. (2011) Uncertainty's Promise. *The Guardian*, 5 February. http://www.guardian.co.uk/commentisfree/belief/2011/feb/05/uncertainty-promise-doubt-science-religion.

CHAPTER 11

Using Your Spiritual Self as a Youth Work Tool

Maxine Green

The approach of this chapter

The classic approach to faith and spirituality is to take a theoretical perspective and to analyse the subject at arm's length. This is a sound theological endeavour but, despite its merits, leaves the reader to make the transition from theoretical knowledge to developing practical knowledge and relevant skills. These two approaches may be encapsulated in the phrases learning about and learning from with the former relating to academic study and the latter to practical, applied learning. This distinction is not new. Plato and Socrates challenged the Sophists and their preoccupation with formulating increasingly complex theory that was separate from everyday life.

In this chapter, I aim to explore the way we as a profession support ourselves and other practitioners in learning from spirituality and spiritual development. While to some extent this includes learning about, starting from a theoretical perspective invites the reader to enter into a safe academic backwater rather than engaging in the more traumatic waters of self-challenge and discovery.

Accordingly, this chapter is my attempt to encourage the reader to learn from exploring themselves and their working practice rather than learning about how one uses one's spiritual self as a youth work tool. Some academic forums and texts do not allow this approach, as it does not display the surface badges of academic authenticity. My background in social anthropology has shown me many endeavours where the initial ethnographic experience is translated into data and rewritten in an academic style. This practice can pull the reader out of the raw experience of the researcher into an observed world with an academic tone and detached judgement. My aim here is to find a style that has rigour, attention and critical judgement but that enables the reader to more directly translate the experience into their own world – to learn from rather than simply learn about. Another factor that has guided my writing of this chapter is that it is modelling the way we develop spiritually. So it is holistic, relates to feeling and doing as well as thinking, and takes advantage of oblique rather than obvious statements so that the mind discovers things rather than is bludgeoned into a sterile understanding. I hope that the reader is able to 'go with' this style of writing.

For those whose want to know more about the subject, I have appended some suggestions for further reading.

Introduction

Many of the social sciences, having a liberal and rationalist value base, have distanced themselves from the concept of spirituality. Youth work, however, has concerned itself with the all-round, or holistic, development of young people. The emphasis on body, mind and spirit epitomised by the YMCA and other pioneer youth work organisations, has been an intrinsic part of youth work values and been carried into the relationships with young people which are a central feature of its approach.

Definitions

The spiritual aspect of such holistic development is the most difficult to define and pin down. Though many people would argue this is the bedrock of a relationship, the intangible nature of spirituality means that it is difficult to describe and hard to validate and so is marginalised as a consequence. The more robust concepts of 'body' and 'mind' can often be demonstrated, measured and defined in terms of outcomes, however imperfect. Spirituality, by contrast, is a multi-faceted, complex concept and its richness may make it appear slippery and indeterminate.

Spirituality is also contentious as it is often conflated with concepts of faith or religion. When spirituality is seen as synonymous with religion, the practices of some religious organisations are impossible to defend in relation to youth work values and practice. Forceful and arrogant proselytising, for example, does not sit readily with notions of empowerment, voluntary engagement and equal opportunities.

Although spirituality is a concept which carries much baggage and leads to misunderstandings, it is very difficult to find an alternative word. One possibility is 'mindfulness' but this has limitations as it does not necessarily include connection with 'the other' which, for many people is a fundamental aspect of their understanding of spirituality. Religious authors have written whole tomes on mindfulness but, in brief, I see mindfulness as limited to a presence of mind with attention to the present moment.

Research on spirituality and spiritual development has identified a cluster of values with associated behaviours that have gained reasonable consensus as being spiritual. Examples of these concepts, which were gathered by Nigel Pimlott, include the words breath, beauty, transcendent, hope, taboo, inwardly turned and love (see Green, 2006: 6–7, for the full list).

Daughtry (2010) utilises the following definition, originally from Engrebretson:

> Spirituality is **experience** of the sacred other which is **accompanied** by feelings of wonder, joy, love, trust and hope. Spirituality **enhances connectiveness** within the self, with others and with the world. Spirituality **illuminates** lived experience. Spirituality **may be expressed** in relationships, prayer, personal and community rituals, values, service, action for justice, connection with the earth. Spirituality **may be named** in new and re-defined ways, or through the beliefs, rituals, symbols, values and stories of religious traditions.
>
> (Engebretson, 2007 cited by Daughtry 2010: 25 with Daughtry's emphasis)

Daughtry draws on Bouma's (2006) work to discuss how the term 'sacred', itself connected to spirituality, may also refer to 'a non-religious disposition that is reflective and attuned to the poetic, aesthetic, psychosocial, imaginative and ethical dimensions of human existence' (Daughtry, 2010: 25).

Although the word spirituality has limitations there seems to be enough shared understanding to go with it in order to explore the very important influence it can play in people's lives. As youth workers are very practical people, the concept of spirituality feeds into how it is articulated in relationships with young people. Youth work is not concerned with 'spirituality, as an idea or concept, but as a praxis . . . a perennial human concern' (King, 1998: 97).

The meaning of spirituality varies across cultures. However, spirituality is equivalent to 'Yeongseong' in Korean. 'Yoengseong' means the nature (seong) of spirit (yeong). It indicates the nature or character of the metaphysical or mental aspects of humanity. It can refer to an ultimate immaterial reality; an inner path enabling a person to discover the essence of one's being; or the supreme values and meanings one seeks. Meditation, contemplation and prayer are considered major spiritual practices for developing an individual's inner life. Through the spiritual practice one could experience enlightenment or connectedness with the ultimate reality. Spirituality is often experienced as a source of inspiration or orientation in life. In general, many religions have regarded spirituality as a core aspect of religious experience. In the world, spirituality has been much related with humanistic character, such as contentment, harmony, compassion, and benevolent care for others. Spiritual experiences transcend materialist views of the world, without necessarily accepting belief in divine being. Meditation and mindfulness can help people find peace and human fulfilment without any religious explanation. Arguably, spirituality in this context is drawn on whenever one seeks the meaning and value of life. Additionally, spirituality encompasses both inner practice and outward service. Compassion, for example, could be understood as the manifestation of spiritual attainment.

The title of this chapter is *Using your spiritual self as a youth work tool*. It is intended to enable an exploration of both the nature of the spiritual self and its deployment in practice with young people. The spiritual self is perceived as embracing a cluster of values and associated behaviours. It is a dimension of one's humanity which is distinct from the mind and the body, but closely interrelated with both of these. The term 'youth work tool' refers to the techniques and processes youth workers bring to inform and articulate their practice. As such, this chapter explores how the 'spiritual self' operates during a youth work encounter and how it can be proactively developed to enhance the relationship between the youth worker and the young person.

Becoming a spiritually reflective practitioner

My argument is that the spiritual self is always present in any relationship, whether acknowledged or not. The beauty of focussing on this aspect is that it can be celebrated and developed. By bringing the skills of reflective practice into the spiritual dimension of a professional relationship, learning and improvement can take place. Spiritual growth moves from being a serendipitous outcome to something that can be warmly and effectively nurtured and encouraged.

When this dimension is vivaciously present in an encounter then good things can happen for the young person and the youth worker. This should not be a side line of youth work, it should be core and central; furthermore young people have a right to this dimension of themselves being attended to and developed. With the spiritual dimension embedded in the youth work experience, the subsequent youth work offer is enriched and enhanced.

The spiritual aspect of accompanying a young person

The report *Youth A Part*, published by the Church of England in 1996, suggested sixteen visions of what the Church could be if young people were to really be a part of it. One of the findings showed the importance of relationship and was expressed in the statement 'We have a vision of a church where youth work is built on good relationships with young people' (Church of England, 1996: 165). A further vision was for the Church to make resources available to support the work with young people (Ibid: 161). The report recognised that church tradition or 'churchmanship' was only a nominal factor in young people feeling included in churches. The age of the volunteer and the particular approach to youth engagement were also not significant defining features. Young people reported that the most important factor that contributed to them feeling included and part of the church was when there was a connected, caring relationship. Through further discussions and correspondence a concept termed 'accompanying' emerged. This was then explored in a separate book called 'Accompanying young people on their spiritual quest' written by Chandu Christian and myself (Green and Christian, 1998).

Techniques are often seen as providing additional competence and skills to a person. The defining feature of 'accompanying' is that it involves the accompanist removing the aspects of their self that get in the way of making a relationship profound and helpful. One of the aspects to set aside when accompanying is the need to transmit knowledge and learning as one would do in a formal mentoring or teaching relationship. The accompanist must quieten their own internal chatter and thus create a powerful 'listening space' where the young person can explore issues and concerns for themselves. The most significant aspect of accompanying is for the accompanist to set aside their own ego and shift their energy to connecting with and being available for the young person.

Various metaphors can be used to describe this process. One is a musical analogy where a tabla player is accompanying a sitar instrumentalist (Green and Christian, 1998). The tabla player waits patiently with their drums for the sitar player to receive 'sruti', or divine inspiration, and then 'holds' the music so that the sitar playing is supported and confirmed. When the sitar player falters, the tabla plays more strongly and with a more obvious beat; when the sitar is strong and confident, the tabla player retreats into the background. This sensitive waiting to hear what is needed and wanted involves mindfulness and concentration. It involves quietening one's inner noise in order to hear exactly where the sitar player is and developing a sensitive and subtle awareness. The ego of the tabla player is not squashed or repressed, the task of listening with this deep, quiet concentration means that the ego is simply redundant and moves aside.

The very best examples of accompanying reveal a similar process. The accompanist is so tuned, stilled and working at a deep and subtle level that their own ego does not feature and they are able to create a safe and meaningful space for the young person to inhabit. This works well when the young person who is accompanied is not only able to occupy, use and grow from accessing this affirmed space but goes on to create it internally on their own initiative. Although this has been described above in terms of listening to words and sounds, accompanying can also happen in silence. When the young person is held in an affirming and hopeful gaze this can sometimes be enough.

Another picture that we used to describe accompanying comes from the etymological root of the word (Green and Christian, 1998). Panis is Greek for bread and com means 'together with' and so the term accompaniment originally refers to the meat or relish used to make the bread tasty and interesting. Similarly if a young person is able to experience this extra dimension it brings a life which is richer, tastier and more exciting (Green and Christian, 1998: 2). Accompanying is not just a specific behavioural technique; it is connecting with the young person at a spiritual level. A youth worker who is able to accompany young people is someone who has begun the process of quietening themselves, shifting the energy from their own ego to being available and tuning in to the spiritual core of the young person.

The benefits to the youth work relationship of the worker being mindful

Youth workers do their job in many ways. Accompanying a young person face-to-face, or working with a small group where there is reflection and concentration, can be approaches where the spiritual nature is actively involved. Spiritual engagement, however, does not necessarily have to happen in quiet situations or in hushed tones. When the sitar player is playing fast and loud and the tabla player drumming with extreme effort and enthusiasm, there is still a link. The tabla accompaniment falls off if the ego of the player takes over and they lead rather than follow the sitar player. Similarly, in carrying out a whole range of youth work activities, the youth worker needs to be tuned into the needs of young people to make them successful.

Mindfulness is a quality which can be used by workers to ensure that they are available and ready to serve young people. This involves being deeply secure within oneself. The state of mindfulness occurs through fully inhabiting the present moment rather than carrying past thoughts and baggage or allowing the mind to race on to tackle things in the future. A mindful person realises that past baggage, or harmful ways of seeing and operating in the world, need to be processed and diffused so that they are no longer carried nor are able to act as a burden or distraction. Mindfulness is achieved when an individual can locate a calm and safe place within themselves which they can readily access. Some people achieve this through prayer but an external God is not necessary to the process. This internal point of stillness has been described by many poets, artists and humanists. Living and working with the capacity to locate this centre means that experience is deeply rooted and has a sound foundation. It is often referred to as being grounded or centred. In this state it is easier to discern what is important and necessary and one can bring careful attention to a situation. This careful attention often reveals the deeper qualities which can open the doors to experiencing awe and wonder. A youth worker taking a group of young people to climb a mountain with a spirit of mindfulness will bring an extra dimension of aspiration and possibility to the event. A youth worker who deeply enjoys music and brings a mindful state to this will communicate at a soulful level the meaning of the music to them. By being moved and open to the music transforming and affecting them, young people can be enriched if they also connect with music and allow it to affect them at a deeper level. A person who has achieved this ability to be mindful is able to bring this quality as a spiritual tool into any youth work situation. A technique I use to support my mindfulness is to imagine my mind as one of those glass globes with a model inside – where you shake the snow and it obscures the scene. I check my mind to see if it is in a state of blizzard and, if it is, quieten it so that the snow falls and I can see clearly.

Supporting young people to access their spiritual selves

Modelling is one of the most powerful tools in encouraging and developing behaviour. If the youth worker has a developed and powerful spiritual life, this will be apparent to young people and they will see its value and impact. This is most easily seen in the context of faith. A Muslim youth worker who attends prayers regularly, observes Ramadan and lives by the values of the Koran will provide an example to young people. Similarly, a Christian youth worker who has a rich prayer life and holds some key Christian values, which may not be those normally held in society, will be seen as offering something different.

It is curious that even in a faith-based context, people are often reluctant to share their faith and spiritual practices. Often they are unsure or unskilled in how to do this rather than unwilling. For example, a sensitive youth worker who has a faith will be reluctant to proselytise and will often step back from sharing their faith to make sure that they are not imposing their beliefs on the young person. However, there are ways of sharing faith and spirituality which are more akin to offering opportunities than simply teaching or programming young people. These embrace the youth work concepts of empowerment, equality of opportunity, education and voluntary engagement. Here the youth worker is very much led by the needs and questions of the young person and is sensitive to sharing ideas, information and practice. A mindful, sensitive and straightforward discussion often works best. Through these discussions, youth workers can sensitively explore with young people the ways in which they are comfortable in exploring their own spirituality and mindfulness and may even develop group practices for this. A technique that Quakers use to help children to still their minds is to have a jar of sand and water in the centre of the circle. The jar is shaken and the children focus on the settling sand as the water clears bringing increased clarity. The Brahma Kumaris (an international spiritual community founded in India in the 1930s) have a practice called 'Just a Minute' or JAM. Every hour, one minute is set aside for reflection and for directing the mind inwards.

Using spiritual concepts to inform youth work

Although faiths or religions do not own important values such as justice, compassion and respect, there have been generations of thinkers and practical people who have explored and articulated these in religious contexts. It is important that the explorations and resources around these concepts are available to young people; they are their heritage and should not be hoarded by the old. Other organisations, which are not necessarily theist, also hold these articulated truths, for example the Humanist Society, the Arts and Crafts movement and the Outdoor Education movement.

It is relatively simple to teach about these values as part of a shared history, where the facts are passed on and the information transmitted. The added element which brings the truths alive is when they are transmitted with spirit, ownership and meaning. People who have lived by these values, and have engaged with the struggle to give meaning to them in their own lives, can be powerful embodiments of the truths they believe in. When they share their stories and their struggles, the experience is embedded and human rather than academic and at arm's length. This encourages those listening to them to associate more fully with the values and there can be a contagion in sharing ideas in this way; to learn from rather than to learn about. Notable contemporary examples include Burma's Aung San Suu Kyi or Tibet's Dalai Lama. A youth work example might be a local youth worker who has been committed to peace. The worker's journey, struggles, achievements and commitment is not just a story of her thinking or her actions; it is a story which is deeply connected to her spirit. The youth worker who has been spiritually engaged in areas of meaning and importance is a powerful example of good living for the young people she works with. Spiritual concepts are part of the heritage of each young person and the articulation of these will enable them to build spiritual resources which can be part of their identity and life.

Managing the ego

In Western countries there is often an emphasis on individual achievement where the 'I' or the ego is praised and rewarded as the driver to effecting change. Spiritual development requires a different approach and many religious traditions involve a simplifying or stripping away of personal clutter. For many people, this sets up a difficult tension in that the concept of Western learning involves gathering and acquiring whereas spiritual learning can be more of a shedding process. This means that the first aspect to manage is the different learning paradigm for spiritual development – one of essentialising and purifying.

A key part of this method is to redefine achievement as deepening understanding so one does not become dependent on praise or criticism. Building an internal reference which measures in terms of effectiveness and compassion encourages an approach to spiritual development which can be observed and reflected on. Shifting from looking for external validation to simple internal measurement helps to shift concentration away from the ego. However, this attempt to deny the ego involves the use of ego to do so. The more one actively engages in 'stamping ego out', the more that one is building the 'good ego' as a power to do this. As such, one ends up constructing a more powerful ego rather than losing their ego.

There are many techniques to shift the energy from the ego to a different goal or task. When one gets engrossed in something, be it making a chair or supporting a young person, the energy flows to the joy of the process and to building a good outcome. In such a situation the ego is more likely to be ignored and not be looking to be fed and noticed. This selflessness is naturally humble and creates more internal space in the youth worker since the ego does not need to be attended or fed. Youth workers who practice this self-lessness have a surer and simpler approach to their work with young people. The goal can be the positive outcomes for the young person with little energy deflected into 'what makes me look good?' or even 'how am I doing?'

The power of doing spiritual 'work' on oneself as a worker and how this can inform youth work

I have a picture of myself as a house. At the top of my house there is an attic with lots of chests and boxes in. I am fearful about what is in some of the chests as some seem locked, so at least once a day, I have to go and check that the chests haven't come undone and the bad things escaped. It takes quite a bit of energy making sure that it is all secure so one by one I open the chests and, with courage, clear the contents out. That way there are no nasty things to surprise me and I don't have to keep on checking to keep myself safe.

It takes courage to be able to see the dark side of one's personality, the part of oneself that one would rather not be there. However, all people have elements of themselves that are unpalatable, which burden us: these parts require energy to contain so that they do not overwhelm our good intentions. A way of managing this is to accept these thoughts and feelings as part of oneself and then hold them up to a spiritual scrutiny whilst caring and loving oneself. In this way the dark internal elements are untangled and placed with acceptance into the broader personality. This process offers a way of clearing out feelings or memories that are not helpful but are being 'carried' and thus take energy and attention. At its very best, there can be a transformation of negative, dark stuff into something powerful, good and wonderful. The resurrection of Jesus or the phoenix stories, of good or beauty arising from destruction, are useful metaphors.

It is important not to underestimate what is involved in this work; it needs inner courage and heart to continue to love oneself when revealing internal dark intentions. This process of inner understanding, love and forgiveness can be extremely healing. Doing this internal work is highly worthwhile as it brings internal freedom and peace. Not only does this make the youth worker more able to give space to others it provides an alternative way of being for young people to see and model. Facing one's inner demons and finding a point of resolution through understanding and hope is extremely empowering. Although this is very personal work, others can sensitively accompany you and encourage your healing.

Issues to manage when working from a spiritual base

According to Noel Burch's model, there are four stages to go through when learning a new skill:

- Unconsciously unskilled
- Consciously unskilled
- Consciously skilled
- Unconsciously skilled

(cited by Adams, 2011: web)

This process is as true for spiritual skills or competence as in other areas where we improve and develop ourselves. One of the problems for people who are skilled, either consciously or unconsciously, is that the environment that they work in may be unconsciously unskilled. This means that an 'unconsciously unskilled' manager of a spiritually mature youth worker may not be able to grasp the purpose of what the youth worker is trying to achieve. The position of being unconsciously unskilled regarding spirituality does not just apply to managers or staff in an organisation; it can also be embedded in its policy and practice. Thus a youth worker who is consciously or unconsciously skilled spiritually can find that their way of working is not valued and, even more so, that it is off the radar of their organisation's approach. A key task for an individual who wants to be proactive with spirituality in their work is to educate those working with them.

Another issue for the youth worker is keeping themselves spiritually growing and developing. Time to reflect, withdraw and study are sometimes difficult to programme into an active timetable. It is also hard to justify these activities within an organisation that does not feature or value spirituality. However, the internal life of the youth worker is so important to the process that it needs to be built in to their working life. Reflective practice is key to building skills, values and behaviours. The cycle of assessing need, planning, doing and evaluating is as effective in building spirituality as in other areas for the youth worker. Identifying spiritual skills and learning how to use them is an important part of building this model of reflective practice. Spiritual skills and behaviours can be part of religious practice; for example through prayer, giving, worship, service, meditation, pilgrimage and social action. Spiritual skills and behaviours independent of religious practice can focus on mindfulness, management of ego or living in accordance with one's values (for example through living simply as a way of supporting the environment or being vegetarian to articulate a belief in the worth of animals).

Summary of how to develop your spiritual self as a youth work tool

- Clear out the baggage in your life that is burdening the way that you see and operate in the world.
- Learn to 'still your soul' so that you have ready access to inner peace and security.
- Learn to distract your ego by concentrating on the task or the young person.
- Take time to reflect, withdraw and study spiritually.
- Work with other people who may be unconsciously unskilled spiritually to develop their knowledge so that they can support your approach.
- Be aware that your own life, values and approach may be used as a model by young people.
- Be part of a community which is consciously and unconsciously skilled about spiritual work and learn and share within this community.
- Be as reflective a practitioner in your spiritual work as you are in other aspects of your work.

Knowing that our spiritual selves are present

Youth work that is approached from a spiritual base has integrity and is values-led rather than behaviour-focussed. The youth worker is able to access inner reserves of strength and positive energy which can provide an anchor while working in chaotic situations. The qualities and values which cluster around the notion of spirituality will be evident in the work. For example, the management and practice of the work will be fair and just. A foundation for the work will be respect for the young people and for others.

Young people in this sort of environment will experience an appreciation of their reflective qualities and of their own searching for truth. They will be encouraged to explore their deeper values and to manifest these within their lives and their identity. They will have access to information and experiences of people who have studied and lived spiritual lives and will have the opportunity to examine these and learn from them. Young people will understand that spiritual living is not just an individual pursuit but takes place in community.

It is probable that this will lead to action such as campaigning, supporting others and working to bring about physical manifestations of spiritual truths.

Conclusion

This chapter contains some concepts which could be construed as fanciful and idealistic. Youth workers are human and make mistakes. The picture summarised above is the ideal of the youth worker working to her full spiritual competence and provides a model for workers to strive for. This notion of the 'unachievable sacred ideal' being something that one can improve themselves by working towards is certainly not alien within discourses of spirituality. This chapter has aimed to explore the concept of utilising one's spiritual self and articulating that concept at work. I would argue that the best youth workers have an inner core of values and a sense of vocation. Not everyone would share the classification of this as spirituality but would probably accept that their work is values-led and inspired. The term spirituality comes with a lot of baggage. Readers are encouraged to consider the deconstructed term and thus connect with the central argument of this chapter by actively articulating the cluster of values which make up spirituality in their own work and their relationships with young people. The call is to encourage self and others to be purposefully reflective in building spiritually tuned and effective youth work. While there is a lot of writing about spirituality and also about youth work practice, there is not much that brings the two together as an active and powerful discipline. Through developing this, we can build a community of practice that ensures spiritually inspired youth work is not just a serendipitous outcome.

References

Adams, L. (2011) *Learning a New Skill is Easier Said than Done.* Gordon Training International. http://www.gordontraining.com/free-workplace-articles/learning-a-new-skill-is-easier-said-than-done/

Church of England (1996) *Youth A Part.* London: National Society/Church House Publishing.

Daughtry, P. (2010). The Benefits of an Integrated Sacred-secular Approach to Youth Worker Training. In Dowson, M. and Devenish, S. (Eds.) *Religion and Spirituality.* Charlotte, NC, USA: IAP.

Green, M. & Christian, C. (1998) *Accompanying Young People on Their Spiritual Quest.* London: Church House Publishing.

Green, M. (2006) *A Journey of Discovery: Spirituality and Spiritual Development in Youth Work.* Leicester: NYA.

King, U. (1998) Spirituality in a Postmodern Age. In King, U. (Ed.) *Faith and Praxis in a Postmodern Age.* London: Cassell.

Further reading

Dunnell, T. (1998) *Twenty First Century Challenge: Some Dreams, Thoughts and Reflections.* Connect Spiritual Development Project, Birmingham: FYT Publications.

Dunnell, T. (2006) *Taking Time Waiting for Green Shoots. A Look at The Basic Elements of Spirituality and Spiritual Development.* Connect Spiritual Development Project, Birmingham: FYT Publications.

Green, M. (1999) The Youth Worker as Converter. In Banks, S. (Ed.) *Ethical Issues in Youth Work.* London: Routledge.

King, U. (2009) *The Search for Spirituality.* Norwich: Canterbury Press.

Pimlott, J., Pimlott, N. and Wiles, D. (2005) *Inspire Too!* Birmingham: FYT publications.

School Curriculum and Assessment Authority (SCAA) (1995) *Spiritual and Moral Development.* Discussion Paper No. 3, London: SCAA Publications.

School Curriculum and Assessment Authority (SCAA) (1996) *Education for Adult Life: The Spiritual and Moral Development of Young People.* Discussion Paper No. 6, London: SCAA Publications.

Sheldrake, P. (1998) *Spirituality and Theology.* London: Darton, Longman and Todd.

Swinton, J. (2001) *Spirituality and Mental Health Care: Rediscovering a Forgotten Dimension.* London: Jessica Kingsley Publishers.

Young, K. (1999) Youth Worker as Guide, Philosopher and Friend. In Banks, S. (Ed.) *Ethical Issues in Youth Work.* London: Routledge.

You may also be interested in reading:

Youth and Policy, issue 65 (1999) – a special issue of the journal on Spirituality that includes articles by Chandu Christian, John Hull, Jeff Astley and Nick Wills among other key commentators on spirituality.

The papers from the 'International Symposium on Religion, Spirituality and Education for Human Flourishing', 24–26 February 2012, Dar Moulay Boubkar, Marrakech, Morocco. Downloadable from: http://ghfp.info/symposium2012/papers.aspx.

CHAPTER 12

Youth Work Concerning Death and Dying

Jess Bishop

Youth workers may avoid talking about death with young people. The Association for Children with Life-threatening or Terminal Conditions (ACT, 2011) stated that 'over 23,500 children and young people in the UK . . . have been diagnosed with a health condition for which there is no hope of cure'. Additionally, Harrison and Harrington (2001) found that 92% of young people experience a 'significant' bereavement before the age of 16. This chapter asks if the generic youth worker allows sufficient space to talk with young people about death. Conversation is often seen as a crucial aspect of youth work practice (Jeffs and Smith, 2005) and allowing space for young people to talk about spirituality is viewed as key to their positive development (Rankin, 2005). This chapter explores three situations in which young people may need support around the issue of death: where a young person is dying; when a young person experiences bereavement or loss; and how a young person examines more general questions about death. It draws from theory and considers the implications for youth work practice.

I was recently invited to join an interdisciplinary team, as a youth work expert, developing a Children and Young People's Palliative Care postgraduate qualification. This role drew on my previous experiences in youth work management, working with young people in the voluntary and statutory sector, work in schools, Christian youth work and targeted work with young carers. Yet, I found myself in a new arena, working alongside medical professionals, with the remit to offer a youth work perspective. In particular, I was there to advocate for the voice of the young person to be heard and for youth work principles and values to be adopted.

This role introduced me to new concepts as well as ones which felt very familiar to youth work, but the research of Bluebond-Langner (1978) into the 'private lives of dying children' caused me to reflect the most. Her research highlighted that often children were not informed that they were dying; in the main, because family members did not want to upset their child. She found, however, that even though they were not 'officially' told, the children were often aware of their diagnosis and consequently felt isolated from their family and medical professionals. They were not able to discuss their concerns and questions about dying for fear that they would upset the family.

This left me with many questions about palliative care with children and young people. I was left considering the implications for the family and the young person or child if they are unable to speak about their illness and potential death. In particular, I was challenged to consider how far they could be involved in medical decisions which affect them, and whether there was a role for a youth worker to complement that of medical professionals. In short, I was left with the question: what could be the youth worker's role with young people who are dying, or anticipating or grieving for the death of a relative or friend?

This chapter also explores the concept of death as a part of spiritual development within youth work. Until recently, spiritual development formed a separate national occupational standard (LLUK, 2008). The spiritual development of young people is now contained within a holistic view of young people's development (LSIS, 2012). The chapter examines working with dying young people, the bereavement support that a generic youth worker can provide and discusses the concept of death education in youth work contexts. My hope is that it will spark debate and discussion amongst youth work practitioners, educators and those who make decisions about practice, policy and funding. The chapter encourages youth workers to reflect on the implications for practice and any actions required to deal with uncertainties, fears and discomfort that they may hold about death and dying.

My own fear, doubt and discomfort about dealing with death with young people still remains; nevertheless, I hope this chapter encourages the reader to push beyond this for the sake of the young person. For youth workers who accompany young people on their life journeys (Green and Christian, 1998) I am hopeful that they also 'have the confidence to be there with them at times of death and loss, when the meaning breaks down and to offer a framework within which the beginnings of a process of meaning reconstruction can occur.'(Batsleer, 2008: 129).

Youth work with young people who are dying

Working in palliative care is a particular specialism for youth workers and is practised in some hospitals such as the Birmingham Children's Hospital and

Nottingham Hospital (NYA, 2009; Hilton et al., 2004). This section examines the place that a generic youth worker may have in supporting a young person who is in need of palliative care.

Together for Short Lives, (formerly The Association of Children and Young People's Palliative Care or, ACT) defines children and young people's palliative care as:

> . . . an active and total approach to care, from the point of diag-
> nosis or recognition throughout the child's life, death and beyond.
> It embraces physical, emotional, social and spiritual elements and
> focuses on enhancement of quality of life for the child/young person
> and support for the family. It includes the management of distress-
> ing symptoms, provision of short breaks and care through death and
> bereavement.
>
> (ACT, 2009: 1)

A youth worker is a valuable addition to a young person's palliative care team. Whether that be based in a hospital or in the community as a worker who already knows that young person. The youth worker and their particular mode of practice holds the potential to enhance their quality of life.

Price and McNeilly (2009) describe two types of conditions, which may require young people to be in receipt of palliative care:

> Life-limiting conditions are those for which there is no reasonable
> hope of cure and from which children or young people will die. Some
> of these conditions cause progressive deterioration, rendering the
> child increasingly dependent on parents and carers. Life-threatening
> conditions are those for which curative treatment may be feasible or
> fail, such as cancer. Children in long term remission or following suc-
> cessful cure due to treatment are not included.
>
> (Price and McNeilly, 2009: vii)

Both life-threatening and life-limiting conditions require young people to receive specialist medical care and attention. There will also be many non-medical staff who are part of the young person's care package such as teachers, social workers, and arts therapists. They should support the young person emotionally, socially and spiritually alongside their medical care.

Pfund and Fowler-Kerry (2010: 109) found that whilst many profession-als perceive what the experiences, fears, wishes and concerns of the child are, children need the opportunity to express these for themselves. They conclude that 'if we are serious about respecting the rights of children then we must explore ways in which their voices can be heard' (2010: 109). Price and McNeilly (2009) suggest that there is still debate about whether to talk to children about death. The issue of truth-telling is still contentious, even thirty years on from Bluebond-Langner's (1978) study that emphasised the feelings of isolation experienced by dying children. A number of key studies agree that children or young people are best supported if they are able to speak with others about their illness and the possibility of death (Carter et al., 2011; Price and McNeilly, 2009).

The field of teenage cancer care offers a range of best practice examples such as the 'Teenage Cancer Trust', 'Jimmy Teens TV' and youth work provision in the form of learning mentors, and activities co-ordinators (Grinyer, 2007). Nevertheless, what about youth work provision for young people who are dying, but do not have cancer? An ACT (2001: 3) report found that 'although young people with cancer are often provided with adequate services there are many young people with other conditions who are not and whose needs are equally great'. This poses a challenge for funders and providers of palliative care, and a vision for creative ways of working with young people regardless of their reason for needing palliative care.

Jeffs and Smith's (2005) approach to working with young people through informal education helpfully promotes the importance of conversation between a young person and a trusted adult. Grinyer (2007) found that specialist care staff, within teenage cancer work, had developed a good rapport with young people that did not just focus on banter. They were able 'to engage at a deeper level and discuss the very real fears and concerns felt by the young people about their illnesses, treatments and futures' (Grinyer 2007: 148). Training staff in ways of communicating effectively with young people is essential if the support young people receive within palliative care work is to be developed.

Brown and Warr (2007) explored alternative forms of communication to direct conversation, and identified drawing, in particular, as a creative and therapeutic way of expressing emotions that are otherwise difficult to address. The use of creative arts, arts therapists and other activities seem to be alternative ways to engage with young people facing their own mortality. Rather than facing death head on, a more indirect approach using art, drama and music may also be familiar territory to many youth workers.

Arguably then, there is a place for youth work approaches within the palliative care of children and young people. A youth work perspective would include: the encouragement of active participation in decision-making from the child or young person (Badham and Davies, 2007); advocating for young people to have a clear involvement in defining their care plan as well as their need for educational, social, emotional and spiritual development. ACT (2001) recommended that young people: are involved in decision-making; are recognised as a 'distinct group'; have support at transition points and are able to grapple with spiritual issues. These findings are strikingly similar to a youth work agenda.

A practical example of this is found in Alice Pyne, a sixteen year old with terminal cancer. She created a blog that featured a 'bucket list' of things to do before she died. She had a media impact, but her purpose was personal:

> *I'm 16 and I have terminal cancer. I've created a bucket list because there are so many things I still want to do in my life . . . some are possible, some will remain a dream. My blog is to document this precious time with my family and friends, doing the things I want to do. You only have one life . . . live it!*
>
> (Pyne, 2012: web)

This young person's drive, ambition and purpose for her future brought hope and understanding to other people going through similar experiences. However, it prompts questions about the support she had and whether other young people also have the social capital to achieve this or would benefit from youth work intervention.

The context for youth work within palliative care

Youth work is often not recognised as a distinct profession within palliative care. Social workers, arts therapists and educators are recognised as part of the inter-professional team that works with young people and families. Schools are often involved in a young person's palliative care plan through engagement with the health care professionals and social workers that are attached to the family. My question therefore is this: is there a place for a youth worker to be involved too? Is there a need for youth work once someone's diagnosis is terminal? Youth work is often about the hopes and dreams of young people. The evidence shows that a young person with a terminal diagnosis has not necessarily lost their passion for life and may need support to fulfil or renegotiate their hopes and dreams. As de Hennezel (2012) puts it when reflecting with one of her dying patients, 'you showed me that it's possible to face one's own death and go on living and giving meaning to one's own life' (de Hennezel, 2012: 8).

There appears to largely be a lack of youth work support for young people who are in need of palliative care. Perhaps an itinerant team of non-medical professionals could work across a region's medical settings and include roles such as activities co-ordinators, hospital youth workers and learning mentors to deliver a 'youth work' approach to support young people?

Implications for reflection

Some youth workers may think that this section is too specialist to be relevant to their role. Most youth workers, however, are keen to put young people at the centre of their work. Therefore, they should consider how they would respond if one of their young people had a terminal diagnosis and what benefits a young person would receive if a youth worker were involved.

Much youth work has a geographical nature to it. It may be possible for a youth worker to play a role at a local hospital or hospice. However, before embarking on any intervention, you will need to consider, perhaps with a colleague, your own feelings or memories about loss as they will influence your potential work with young people in this arena. Thompson (2005: 119) encourages us to develop, rather than a stoic or 'macho' response to feelings, an 'ethos of permission'. Allowing youth workers to be supportive and open to one another, and not discouraging the discussion of feelings at work, is likely to enable young people to be more effectively supported. It can often be assumed that youth workers are resilient and able to bounce back from the everyday stresses of the work; but burnout should not be underestimated (Thompson, 2005: 119). Take time to also consider how your organisation's approach to feelings, the value of supervision and the balance of stoicism versus permission affects your own response to handling your own and others' feelings within youth work.

Bereavement support for young people from a youth worker

Most people experience bereavement at some point whilst growing up. Harrison and Harrington (2001) indicate that 92% of young people experience a 'significant' loss or bereavement before the age of 16. This suggests that bereavement is a key feature in many young people's lives. However, Allen (1990) noted that, in the late twentieth century, society had only recently acknowledged that children grieve.

Reid and Westergaard (2011) suggest that young people should be referred to a specialist worker if their own youth worker is not trained specifically in bereavement counselling. But is there a place for the universal or generic youth worker to support bereaved young people alongside this specialist support? A youth worker who already has a trusting relationship with a young person, and has considered the subject in some depth, could be ideally placed.

A number of specialist organisations that offer support to children, young people, carers and parents also provide training for professionals working with children and young people. These organisations include: Winston's Wish, the 'largest provider of services to bereaved children, young people and their families in the UK' (Winston's Wish, 2012: web); Guy's Gift, a bereavement charity providing support to children, young people and their families in South Warwickshire (Guy's Gift, 2012) and This Way Up, a Christian charity that delivers support through schools to young people who are experiencing difficulties due to loss, bereavement or parental separation (This Way Up, 2012). All three examples offer positive approaches to support young people as they experience grief, loss and bereavement. It is recommended that a strengths-based approach to supporting bereaved young people is beneficial. For example, Mallon refers to resilience research that 'seeks to find out what sources of strength and positive strategies help the young people adapt to loss' (Mallon, 2011: 9).

Through interviews with people who were terminally ill, Kubler-Ross (1973) presented the coping mechanisms used by dying patients. This model of grief consists of five stages: Denial, Anger, Bargaining, Depression and Acceptance. It is worth noting that Kubler-Ross (1973: 126) found that whilst the five stages pass, or exist side-by-side, hope usually 'persists' throughout. There has been some debate about Kubler-Ross's model, specifically the linear nature of it, and other theories and models have since emerged. Mallon (2011: 4) introduces youth workers to a number of these including William Worden's task model: a series of tasks must be completed following bereavement including acceptance, 'working through the pain of grief', adjustment, and moving on with life. Spirituality has also been found to be a coping mechanism for grieving children (Andrews and Marotta, 2005). Thompson (2011) indicates that without a basic understanding of grief theory, we could be putting young people in danger. It would therefore be advisable for youth workers to equip themselves with some knowledge before the occasion arises that they may need it.

Mainstream youth work texts such as Sapin (2008), Robb (2007) and Jeffs and Smith (2010) do not have an emphasis on bereavement or death.

Faith-based youth work texts sometimes deal with death in relation to Jesus for example (Fields, 2002; Nash, 2011) or life after death (Khan, 2013). But in the main, they also neglect to deal with a youth worker's practical response to death or bereavement (Fields, 2002; Nash, 2011) with the exception of a practical response to the Bridgend Suicides (Saunders, 2013). Coming from either a theoretical or practice perspective, it seems that the idea of a non-specialised youth worker focusing on bereavement is not a key consideration. In contrast, Batsleer and Davies (2010), Henderson et al. (2010), Lodico and Voegtle (2005) and Krueger (2004) include case studies and the voices of young people in their writing and bereavement is noticeably featured within the stories of the young people they choose to write about (although it should be noted that whilst these texts focus on young people, they are not all 'youth work' texts specifically). Henderson et al. (2010) collected data from young people over a ten-year period about employment, culture and well-being. One key element they draw out in their analysis was the concept of 'critical moments' in young people's lives after events such as divorce, bereavement or bullying, and the impact this may have in the longer term both positively and negatively (2010: 20). They concluded that, 'the most valuable material collected in this study has been accidental such as the accounts of experiences such as bereavement' (2010: 166). Therefore, if young people are not afraid to talk about death, do we offer enough space for them to share the feelings, experiences and questions that come with loss and how might youth workers go about offering that space? In youth work education, reflective practice is considered to be beneficial for youth workers' development and allows the opportunity to take a step back from critical incidents or critical moments in youth work (Emslie, 2009). Reflective practice is taught to youth workers, but is it also applied with young people? In the context of death and bereavement, it is important to consider how reflective practice techniques might help youth workers to create space for young people to identify and express their feelings.

Linking bereavement to spirituality, Batten and Oltjenbruns (1999) found that adolescent sibling bereavement is a catalyst for spiritual development. Should bereavement support thus be regarded as contributing to young people's spiritual development? As Rankin (2005) found, we often do not have the answers but our role should be to provide the space for young people to talk and to be listened to.

For youth workers who find themselves involved in work on bereavement and loss, Mallon (2011) is a useful text. Taking an approach similar to counselling, it covers both the theories of grief (Kubler-Ross's among others) and the practical skills needed in bereavement support. Respect, honesty, accept-ance, confidentiality, empathy, active listening and managing group work with young people are all skills that Mallon suggests a youth worker can uti-lise when working with young people who are bereaved. For those working in a school setting, there is some discussion about educational approaches, protocol and practical tools to use when responding to a death as a whole school. Mallon also addresses the spiritual dimensions of grief and rituals that may help young people who are bereaved. She includes reflexive exercises at the end of each chapter to encourage practitioners to consider their own role and that of their organisation in supporting those who are bereaved. Finally, Mallon (2011) points towards other resources, websites and organisations that can offer advice, support or training.

Youth workers may feel out of their comfort zone and bereavement sup-port can be draining on anyone involved. Thompson (2011: 100) recommends that 'self care needs to be relentless, in the sense that it is not something we can afford to let slip'. Supervision from an understanding manager can be crucial to ensure that a youth worker does not burn out. If a youth worker does not feel able to support a young person through bereavement due to their own experiences of loss it is important to make that clear and refer the young person on. Brown and Warr (2007) emphasise, however, that young people will feel more comfortable talking to an adult they already know. 'Self care' (Thompson, 2011) and addressing our feelings (Thompson, 2005) should be part of our regular practice as youth workers; using reflective practice tech-niques to raise awareness of anything that needs addressing.

Bereavement provision and other supportive policies within youth services vary a great deal. Similarly, recent research has identified that many schools feel they have a training gap on bereavement support for children and that some teachers would rate themselves as underprepared (Holland, 2008). If schools are aware that this is a gap in the support they are able to offer effectively, then it is more crucial that youth workers and youth services also engage in further training on the issue (Cruse Bereavement Care, 2012).

Bereaved young people are likely to experience feelings that are difficult to deal with. They may also experience bullying or isolation from peers and, in extreme cases, may be at risk of harm from family members (Ribbens McCarthy, 2007). It is worth noting, however, that the response to bereave-ment is not always entirely negative. Ribbens McCarthy and Jessop (2005) describe it more as a 'change'. It seems clear that most youth workers are unlikely to seek out bereavement work, but should feel able to respond to and support young people when it occurs, as well as to refer them on when they need more specialist support. The youth work skill-set of practical activities can be useful to draw on; young people often feel able to express their feelings through creative arts. Mallon (2011) suggests that writing diaries and journals, drawing and painting, photography and film making, memory boxes, clay work and memory stones are activities which young people can be guided through in groups or as individuals. Ultimately, however, our ability to work with bereaved young people is down to our own relationship with them and 'our sensitivity, compassion, care and our ability to hold strong emotions and to contain the pain may help the bereaved to travel through their grief' (Mallon, 2011: 11).

Implications for youth work

Youth work key texts and training should include more discussion about bereavement, loss and death as part of the developmental responsibility youth workers have. Bereavement is a prevalent issue facing many young people before they are 16 and will likely face all of us at some point. Youth workers need to remember 'self care' as a matter of priority in order to prevent burn out (Thompson, 2011).

The idea of youth workers offering bereavement support as suggested here brings up some key issues for reflection. First, it needs to be considered whether such a role is a specialist one or should be included within the training and skill-set of all workers. Secondly, the links between bereavement work and spiritual development require fuller reflection, not least for youth workers in faith-based settings. Youth workers need to consider whether they are prepared to handle issues of bereavement and, if not, what they can do to be readier to respond.

Spirituality of death or death education: should they feature in the youth work curriculum?

Can youth workers prepare for death by including the spirituality of death and 'death education' within the youth work curriculum? This is a contentious issue within school settings and there are differences of opinion between children, teachers and theorists (Bowie, 2000). A third of children think death education should be included in school curricula, teachers think death should be 'discussed as the need arises' and theorists believe that teachers should help children 'develop a healthy attitude towards death, while preparing them for future losses' (Bowie, 2000: 25). Where schools are keen to positively address the subject of death, many teachers are not keen to take on the role of co-ordinator (Ribbens McCarthy, 2006). Is this something a youth worker could or should take on as part of their role?

All youth workers have a remit to support young people to develop spiritually. Faith-based youth workers often have this as their main focus whereas other youth workers include spirituality if there is a requirement or interest. However, spirituality can be seen as an uncomfortable subject that many workers shy away from (Green, 2006). The same can be said for death. Incorporating death with spirituality gives an opportunity for youth workers to cover death as part of a youth work curriculum. However, it also needs to be recognised that joining two taboo subjects together could be problematic.

Batsleer (2008: 128) acknowledges that existential questions about life purpose are of 'great urgency for many [young] people'. Death and spirituality are subjects that youth workers are often apprehensive about addressing with young people (Batsleer, 2008; Adams et al., 2008; Lamont, 2007). However, young people do feel comfortable talking about death and seek the space to do so where people are there to listen to their concerns (Hay and Nye, 2006; Hyde, 2008). Luxmoore (2000) argues that as youth workers, we are often reluctant to:

> . . . encourage teenagers just to think about meaninglessness, maybe for fear that they'll lapse into apathy or depression but maybe also because of our own fear of death and meaninglessness. If we've spent our lives creating distractions so as not to think about these things, then a philosophical teenager disturbs it all. So the question is slapped down, the questioner made to feel like a time-waster.
>
> (Luxmoore, 2000: 15)

A faith-based youth worker may more often talk about death in regards to religion and the various perspectives about what happens after death. This may be a natural way in to discuss and pick up any questions that young people may have. However, this may not be as easy to integrate within non-faith youth work or in a setting that is highly activity-based or that occurs only once a fortnight. Luxmoore (2012: 20) encourages youth workers to support young people to wonder about life and death 'openly and often'.

Final thoughts

Youth work is currently concerned with its own demise in a context of wide-spread cuts to youth services. The decrease in funding for youth work on a national scale raises questions about the capacity and willingness of youth workers to think about such wider issues with young people, particularly as youth work faces its own potential 'death'. Vickers (2009) suggests that often workers display similar reactions to redundancy as can be seen for grief.

Youth workers need to consider how far they concur with the concerns teachers have about including death education within the curriculum or whether the more fluid and responsive nature of youth work has greater potential to help young people develop a healthy attitude to death. My hope is that this chapter will have encouraged further reflection and research. More importantly, I hope that such reflection will lead to local action to improve youth work support for young people who are experiencing issues related to death, dying or bereavement.

References

Adams, K., Hyde, B. and Woolley, R. (2008) *The Spiritual Dimension of Childhood*. London: Jessica Kingsley.

Allen, L. (1990) Working with Bereaved Teenagers. In Morgan, C. (Ed.) *The Dying and the Bereaved Teenager*. Philadelphia: The Charles Press.

Andrews, C. and Marotta, S. (2005) Spirituality and Coping Among Grieving Children: A Preliminary Study. *Counselling and Values*, Oct., 50, 38–50.

Association for Children with Life-threatening or Terminal Conditions (2001) *Palliative Care For Young People Aged 13–24 Years*. Bristol: ACT.

Association for Children with Life-threatening or Terminal Conditions (2009) *Children's Palliative Care Definitions*. Bristol: ACT.

Association for Children with Life-threatening or Terminal Conditions (2011) *Children's Palliative Care Handbook for GPs*. Bristol: ACT.

Badham, B. and Davies, T. (2007) The Active Involvement of Young People. In Harrison, R., et al. (Eds.) *Leading Work With Young People*. London: Sage.

Batsleer, J. (2008) Info*rmal Learning in Youth Work*. London: Sage.

Batsleer, J. and Davies, B. (2010) *What is Youth Work?* Exeter: Learning Matters.

Batten, M. and Oltjenbruns, K. (1999) Adolescent Sibling Bereavement as a Catalyst For Spiritual Development: A Model For Understanding. *Death Studies*, Sept. 23: 6, 529–46.

Bluebond-Langner, M. (1978) *The Private Worlds of Dying Children*. New Jersey: Princeton University Press.

Bowie, L. (2000) Is There a Place For Death Education in The Primary Curriculum? *Pastoral Care in Education,* 18: 1, 22–6.

Brown, E. and Warr, B. (2007) *Supporting The Child and The Family in Paediatric Palliative Care*. London: Jessica Kingsley.

Carter, B., Levetown, M. and Friebert, S. (2011) *Palliative Care For Infants, Children and Adolescents: A Practical Handbook*. Baltimore: John Hopkins University Press.

Cruse Bereavement Care (2012) *Cruse Bereavement Care*. http://www.crusebereavementcare.org.uk.

Emslie, M. (2009) Researching Reflective Practice: A Case Study in Youth Work Education. *Reflective Practice,* 12: 3, 323–36.

Fields, D. (2002) *Your First Two Years in Youth Ministry: A Practical and Personal Guide to Starting Right.* Grand Rapids: Zondervan.

Green, M. and Christian, C. (1998) *Accompanying Young People on Their Spiritual Quest.* London: Church House Publishing.

Green, M. (2006) *A Journey of Discovery: Spirituality and Spiritual Development in Youth Work.* Leicester: NYA.

Grinyer, A. (2007) *Young People Living With Cancer: Implications For Policy and Practice.* Berkshire: The Open University and McGraw-Hill Education.

Guy's Gift (2012) *Guy's Gift.* http://guysgift.co.uk/.

Harrison, L. and Harrington, R. (2001) Adolescents' Bereavement Experiences: Prevalence, Association With Depressive Symptoms and Use of Services. *Journal of Adolescence,* 24: 2, 159–69.

Hay, D. and Nye, R. (2006) *The Spirit of the Child.* London: Jessica Kingsley.

Henderson, S., et al. (2010) *Inventing Adulthoods: A Biographical Approach to Youth Transitions.* London: Sage.

de Hennezel, M. (2012) *Seize the Day.* London: Pan Macmillan.

Hilton, D. et al. (2004) Youth Work in Hospital. *Paediatric Nursing,* 16: 1, 36–9.

Holland, J. (2008) How Schools Can Support Children Who Experience Loss and Death. *British Journal of Guidance and Counselling,* 36: 4, 411–24.

Hyde, B. (2008) *Children and Spirituality: Searching for Meaning and Connectedness.* London: Jessica Kingsley.

Jeffs, T. and Smith, M.K. (2005) *Informal Education: Conversation, Democracy and Learning.* Nottingham: Educational Heretics Press.

Jeffs, T. and Smith, M.K. (2010) *Youth Work Practice.* Basingstoke: Palgrave MacMillan.

Khan, M.G. (2013) *Young Muslims, Pedagogy and Islam: Contexts and Concepts.* Bristol: The Policy Press.

Krueger, M. (2004) *Themes and Stories in Youth Work Practice.* New York: Haworth Press.

Kubler-Ross, E. (1973) *On Death and Dying.* London: Routledge.

Lamont, R. (2007) *Understanding Children, Understanding God.* London: SPCK.

Learning and Skills Improvement Service (2012) *Youth Work National Occupational Standards.* LSIS.

Lifelong Learning UK (2008) *National Occupational Standards for Youth Work.* LLUK.

Lodico, M. and Voegtle, K. (2005) *Child and Adolescent Life Stories: Perspectives From Youth, Parents and Teachers.* London: Sage.

Luxmoore, N. (2000) *Listening to Young People in School, Youth Work and Counselling.* London: Jessica Kingsley.

Luxmoore, N. (2012) *Young People, Death and The Unfairness of Everything.* London: Jessica Kingsley.

Mallon, B. (2011) *Working With Bereaved Children and Young People.* London: Sage.

Nash, S. (Ed.) (2011) *Youth Ministry: A Multi-faceted Approach.* London: SPCK.

NYA (2009) *The National Youth Agency Working With Hospital Based Youth Workers in The UK From 2008–09 Under S64 Funding.* Leicester: National Youth Agency.

Pfund, R. and Fowler-Kerry, S. (2010) *Perspectives on Palliative Care For Children and Young People: A Global Discourse.* Oxford: Radcliffe.

Price, J. and McNeilly, P. (2009) *Palliative Care For Children and Families: An Interdisciplinary Approach.* Basingstoke: Palgrave MacMillan.

Pyne, A. (2012) *Alice's Bucket List.* http://alicepyne.blogspot.co.uk/.

Rankin, P. (2005) *Buried Spirituality.* Salisbury: Sarum College Press.

Reid, H. and Westergaard, J. (2011) *Effective Counselling With Young People.* Exeter: Learning Matters.

Ribbens McCarthy, J. and Jessop, J. (2005) *The Impact of Bereavement and Loss on Young People.* York: Joseph Rowntree Foundation.

Ribbens McCarthy, J. (2006) *Young People's Experiences of Loss and Bereavement.* Berkshire: The Open University/McGraw Hill Education.

Ribbens McCarthy, J. (2007) 'They All Look as if They're Coping, But I'm Not': The Relational Power/Lessness of Youth in Responding to Experiences of Bereavement. *Journal of Youth Studies,* 10: 3, 285–303.

Robb, M. (2007) *Youth in Context: Frameworks, Setting and Encounters.* London: Sage.

Sapin, K. (2008) *Essential Skills for Youth Work Practice.* London: Sage.

Saunders, M. (2013) *Youth Work from Scratch: How to Launch or Revitalize a Church Youth Ministry.* Oxford: Monarch Books.

This Way Up (2012) *Helping Young People Turn Their Lives The Right Way Up.* http://twup.org.uk/pro/home.

Thompson, N. (2005) Handling Feelings. In Harrison, R. and Wise, C. (Eds.) *Working with Young People.* London: The Open University/Sage.

Thompson, N. (2011) *Grief and its Challenges.* Basingstoke: Palgrave MacMillan.

Vickers, M. (2009) Journeys Into Grief: Exploring Redundancy For a New Understanding of Workplace Grief. *Journal of Loss and Trauma,* 14, 401–19.

Winston's Wish (2012) *For Young People.* http://www.winstonswish.org.uk/foryoungpeople/default.asp?section=000100010001&pagetitle=Young+People.

Working with street children
An approach explored

By Andrew Williams

'A book that bridges the gap between academia and know-how.' *Andy Sexton, Associate International Director, Oasis Global, Co-chair 180 Degree Alliance.*

Provides an insight into the work involved – and level of commitment demanded – from anyone working with street children in developing countries anywhere. Based on his work as a very locally involved CEO of Retrak in Africa, British social worker Andy Williams provides an analysis of how one approach was tried, tested, improved and expanded through careful and constant attention to reflective analysis and review; and shows how principles can be drawn out which transcend both culture and the practical application of those principles in any one context. The approach is holistic, relational, transitional, child-centred and professional.

'An introductory text book to a brilliant approach drawing on lots of wisdom and experience.' *Youthwork.*

2011 978-1-905541-80-5

Essays in the history of youth and community work

Discovering the past

Edited by Ruth Gilchrist, Tony Jeffs, Jean Spence and Joyce Walker

2009   978-1-905541-45-4

Reflecting on the past

Essays in the history of youth and community work

*Edited by Ruth Gilchrist, Tracey Hodgson, Tony Jeffs, Jean Spence,
Naomi Stanton and Joyce Walker*

2011   978-1-905541-73-7

Young people in post-conflict Northern Ireland

The past cannot be changed, but the future can be developed

Edited by Dirk Schubotz and Paula Devine

Covers not just what we expect to hear when NI is being discussed: violence, sectarianism, faith-segregated schooling, cross-community contact, politics, peace process. But also: inward migration, mental health, suicide, bullying, pupil participation, sexual health, poverty, class, and how best to find out about these things in robust ways that involve young people in shaping the process. It includes the prize-winning essay from a 16-year old: Is Anybody Listening?

'The message of the book is that we have a lot to learn from our youth, if we take the trouble to listen to them' The contribution they make, when they are consulted, can help society with endemic problems such as bullying. The research also shows that the roots of some problems lie in the attitudes young people develop through lack of adequate information.' Therapy Today.

Includes:
Shared or scared? Attitudes to community relations among young people 2003–7
   Duncan Morrow
Adolescent mental health in Northern Ireland: empirical evidence from the Young Life and Times Survey
   Katrina Lloyd, Ed Cairns, Claire Doherty & Kate Ellis
Tackling bullying in schools: the role of pupil participation
   Ruth Sinclair
Honesty about sex and relationships – it's not too much to ask for
   Simon Blake
Diversity or diversion? Experiences of education in Northern Ireland
   Tony Gallagher
Young people's thoughts on poverty
   Alex Tennant & Marina Monteith
Is anybody listening?
   Shaun Mulvenna
Giving young people a voice via social research projects: methodological challenges
   Dirk Schubotz & Paula Devine

2008   978-1-905541-34-8

Reappraisals

Essays in the history of youth and community work

Edited by Ruth Gilchrist, Tony Jeffs, Jean Spence, Naomi Stanton, Aylssa Cowell, Joyce Walker and Tom Wylie

The range of material in this volume reflects the editors' hope to encourage practitioners and academics to reflect upon the earlier forms of practice and, via that process, reappraise what they are currently doing within both fieldwork and teaching.

2013   978-1-905541-88-1